RECORDED VERSIONS GUITAR

AUTHENTIC TRANSCRIPTIONS
WITH NOTES AND TABLATURE

VERY BEST
MICHAEL SCHENKER

Cover photo by Glen LaFerman

ISBN 978-1-4234-0058-5

HAL•LEONARD® CORPORATION

7777 W. BLUEMOUND RD. P.O. BOX 13819 MILWAUKEE, WI 53213

Visit Hal Leonard Online at
www.halleonard.com

Are You Ready to Rock

Words and Music by Michael Schenker and Gary Barden

Solo

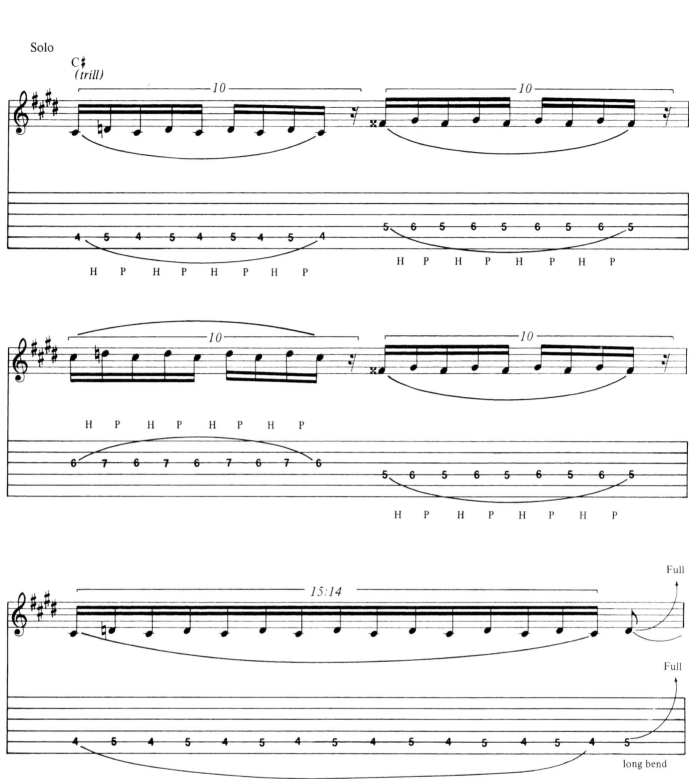

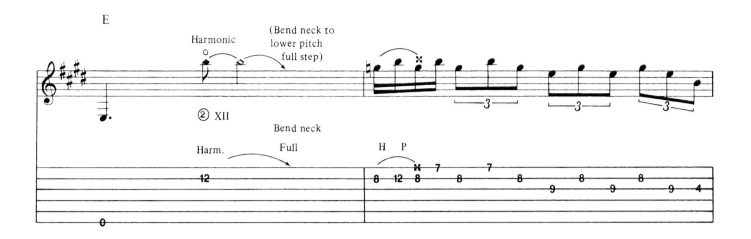

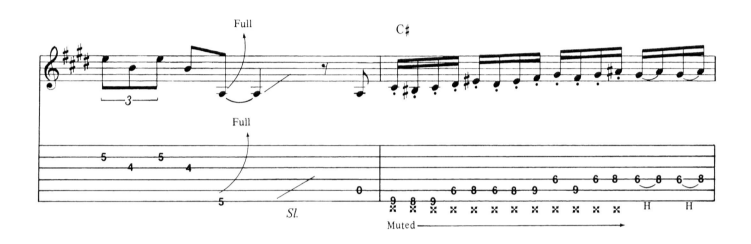

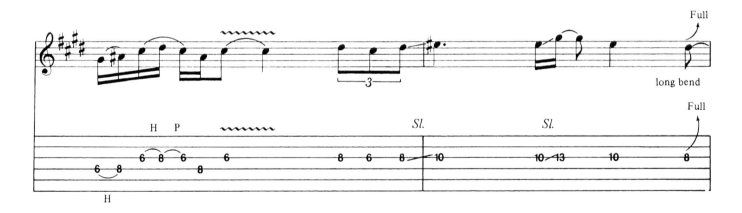

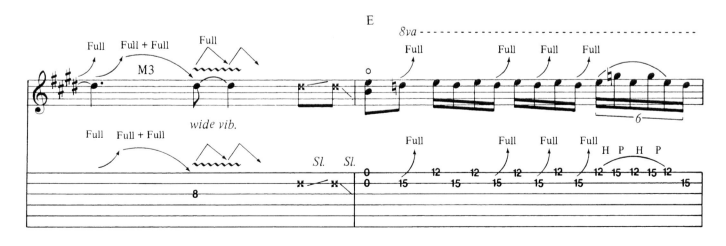

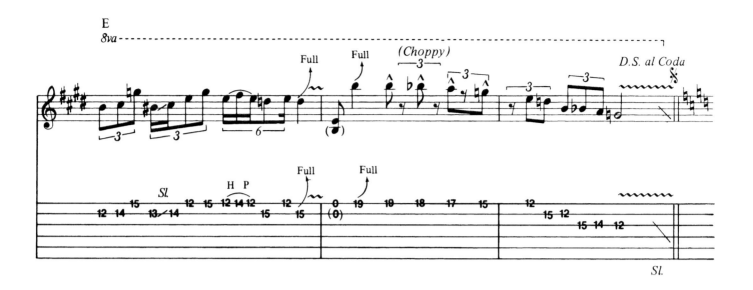

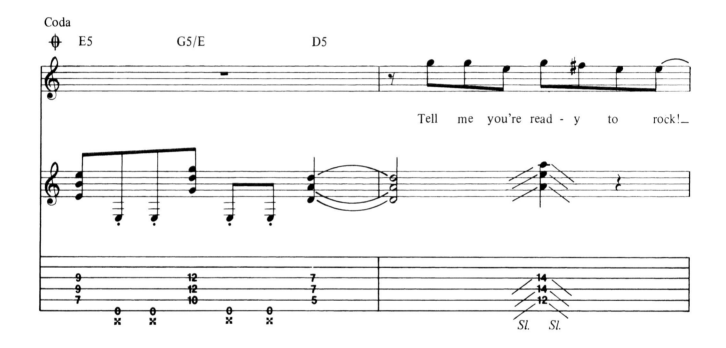

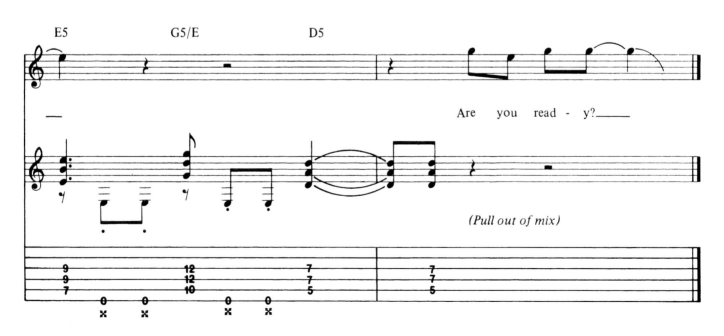

Armed and Ready

Words and Music by Michael Schenker and Gary Barden

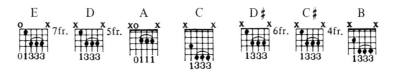

Fast Rock beat
Intro
Main riff

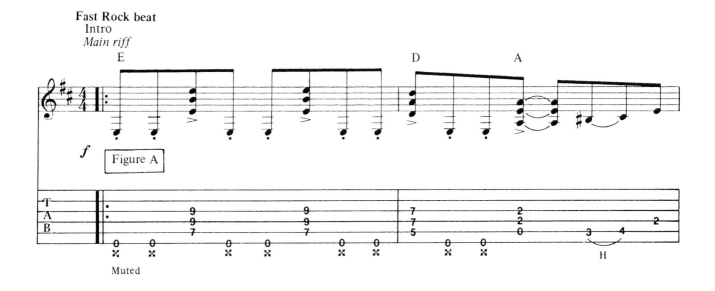

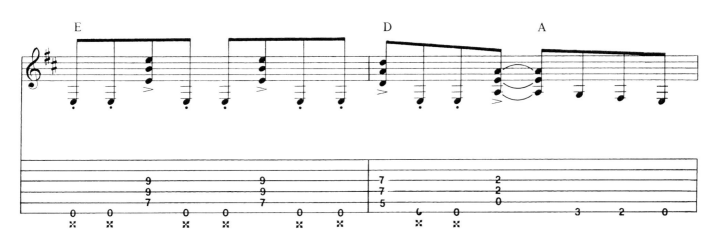

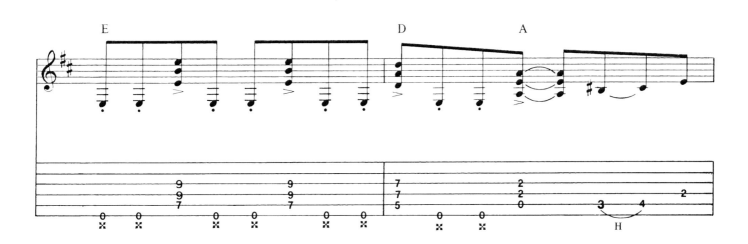

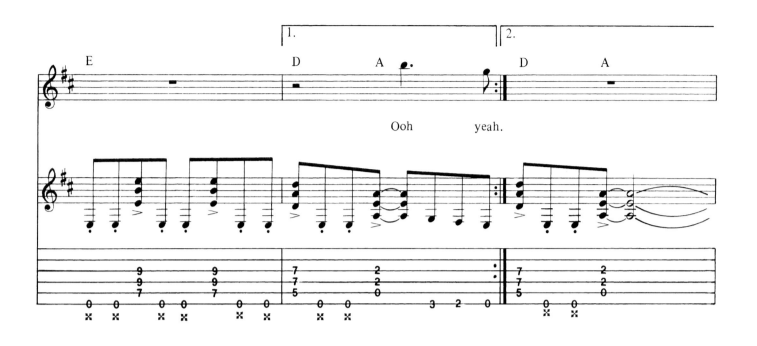

Ooh yeah.

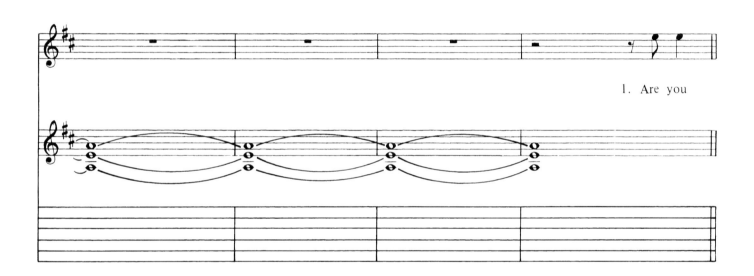

1. Are you

Verse
Fig. A

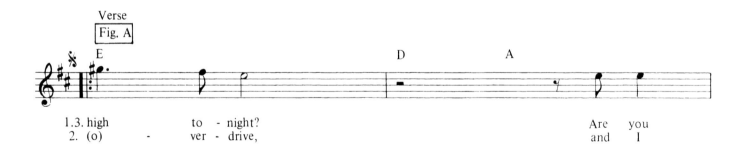

1.3. high   to - night?   Are   you
2. (o)   -   ver - drive,   and   I

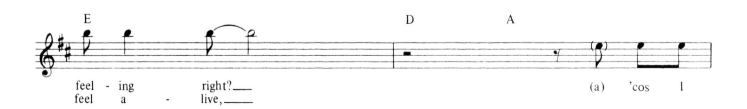

feel - ing   right?___   (a) 'cos I
feel   a   -   live,___

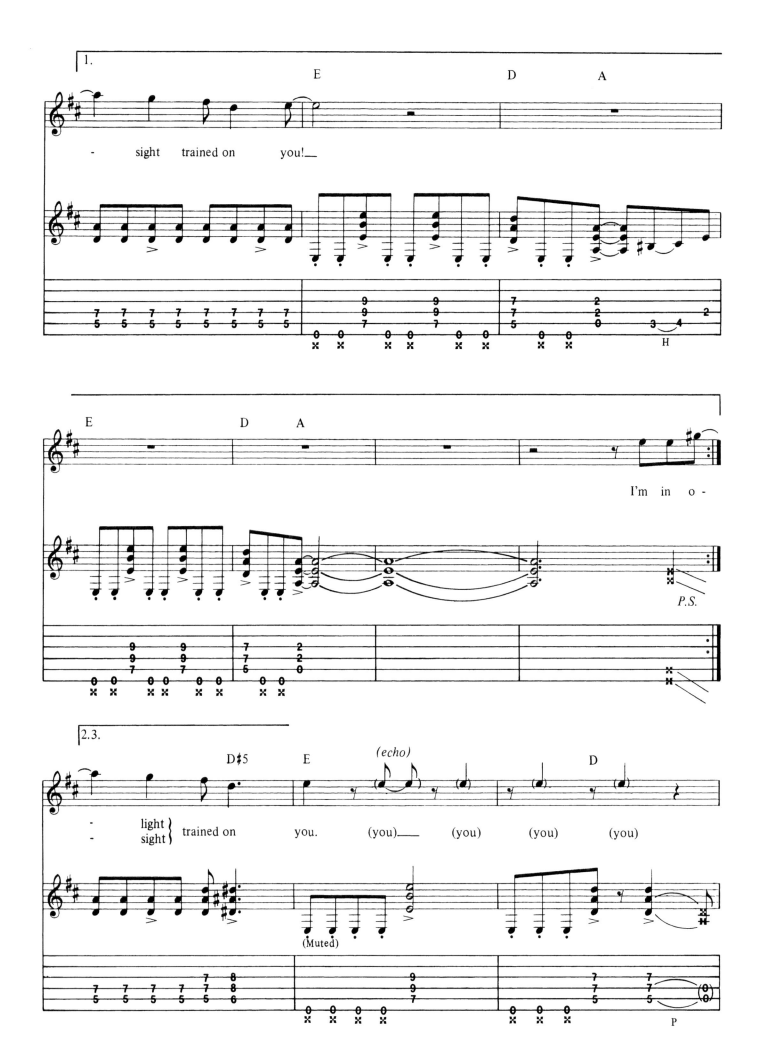

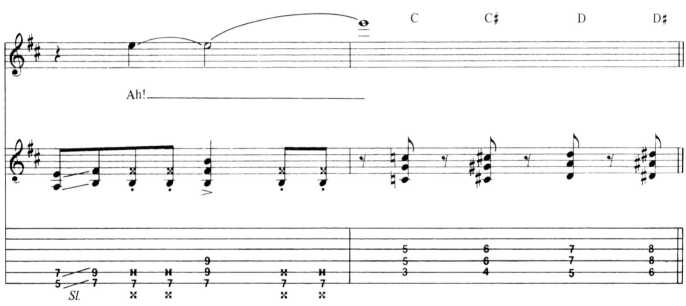

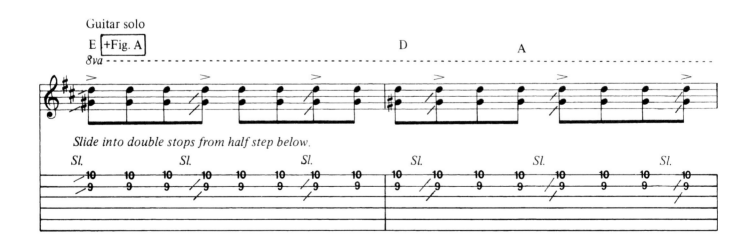

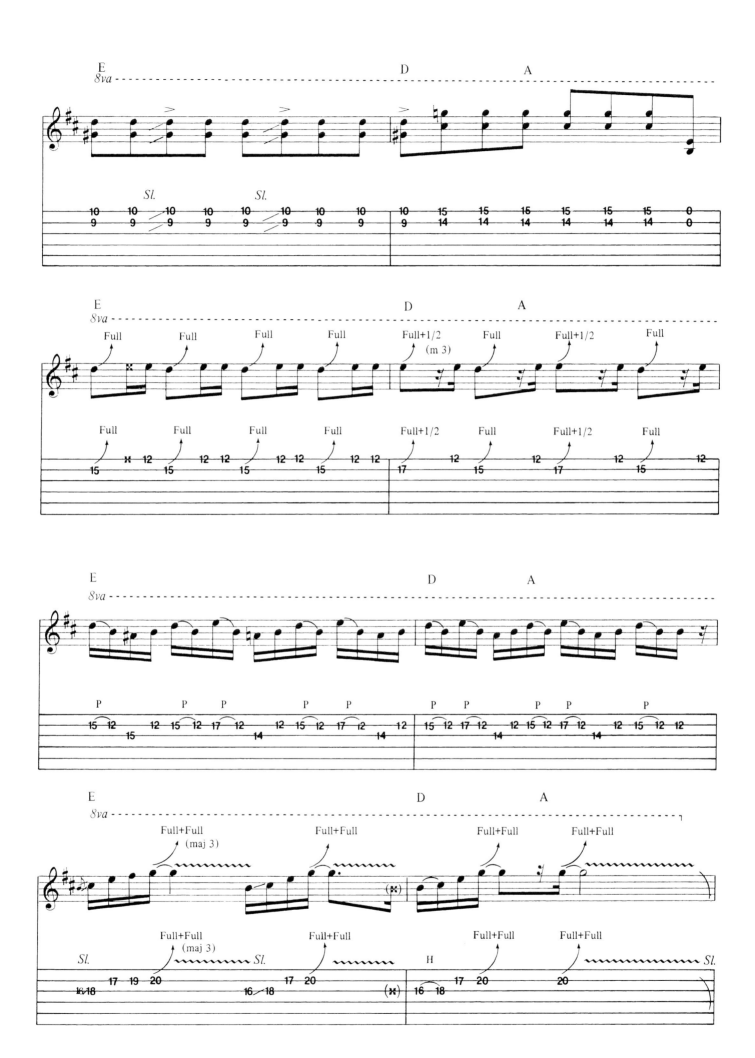

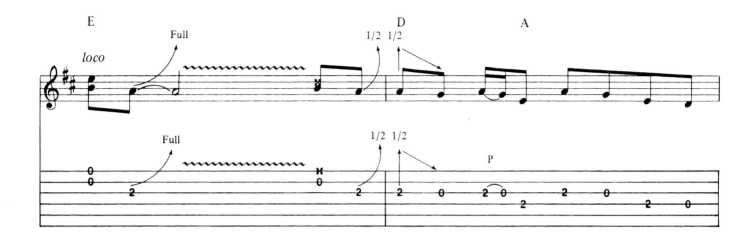

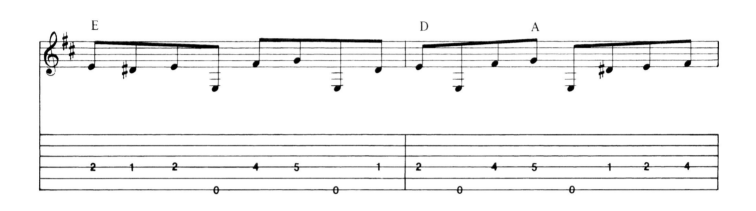

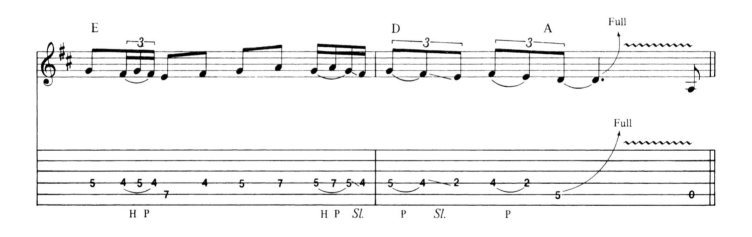

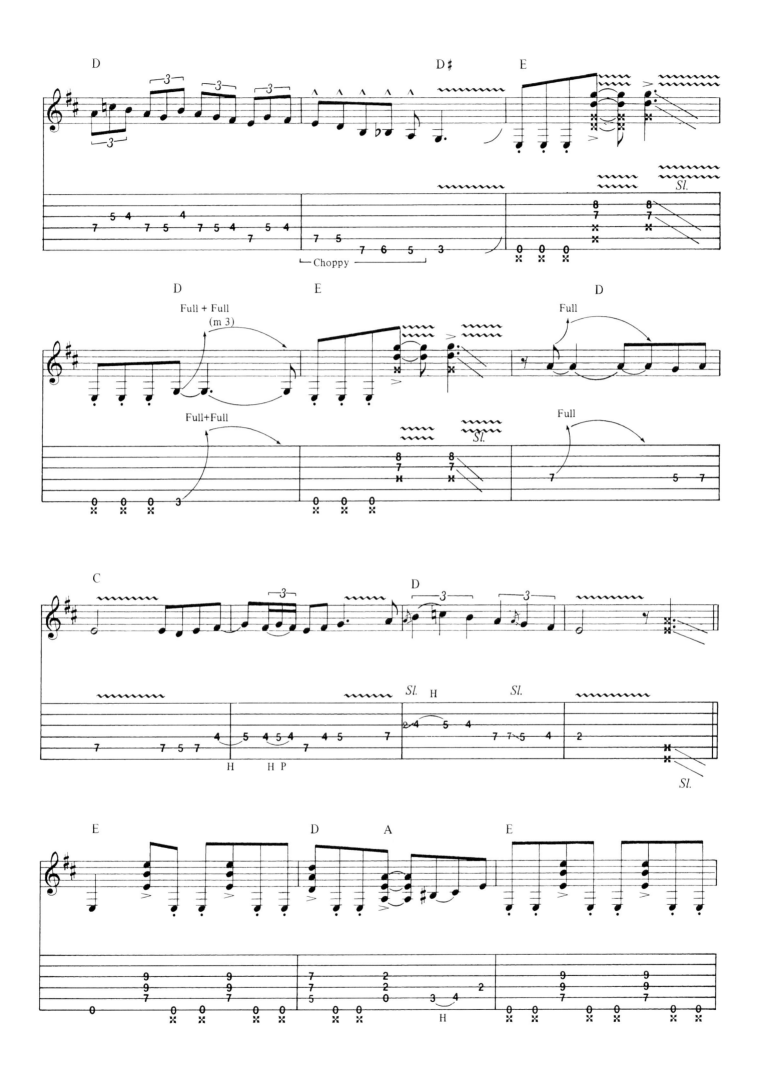

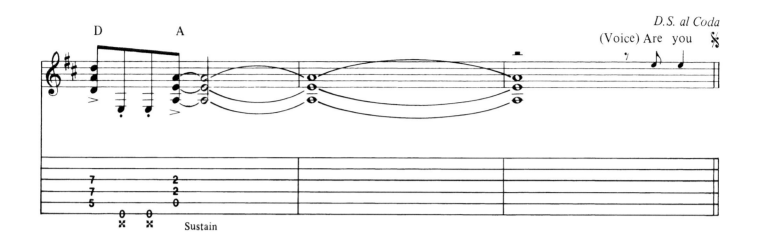

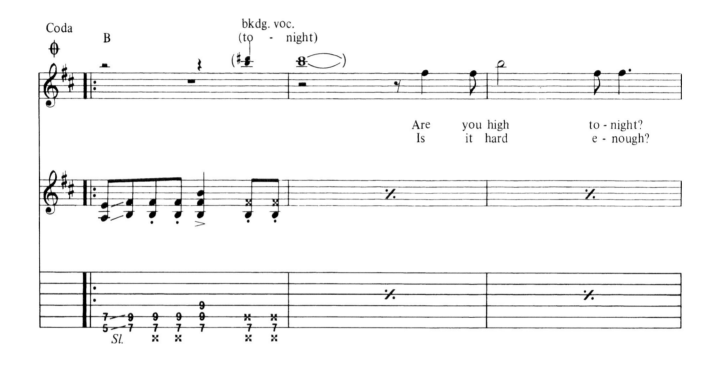

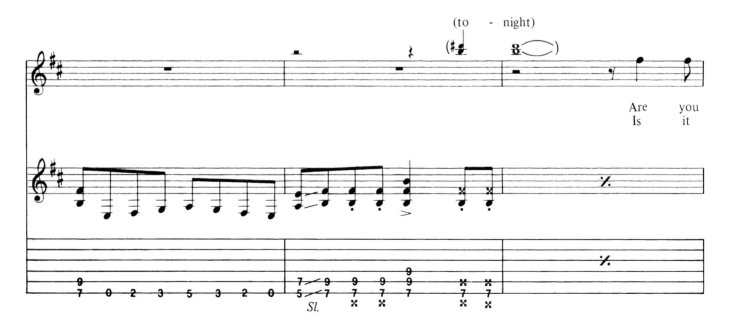

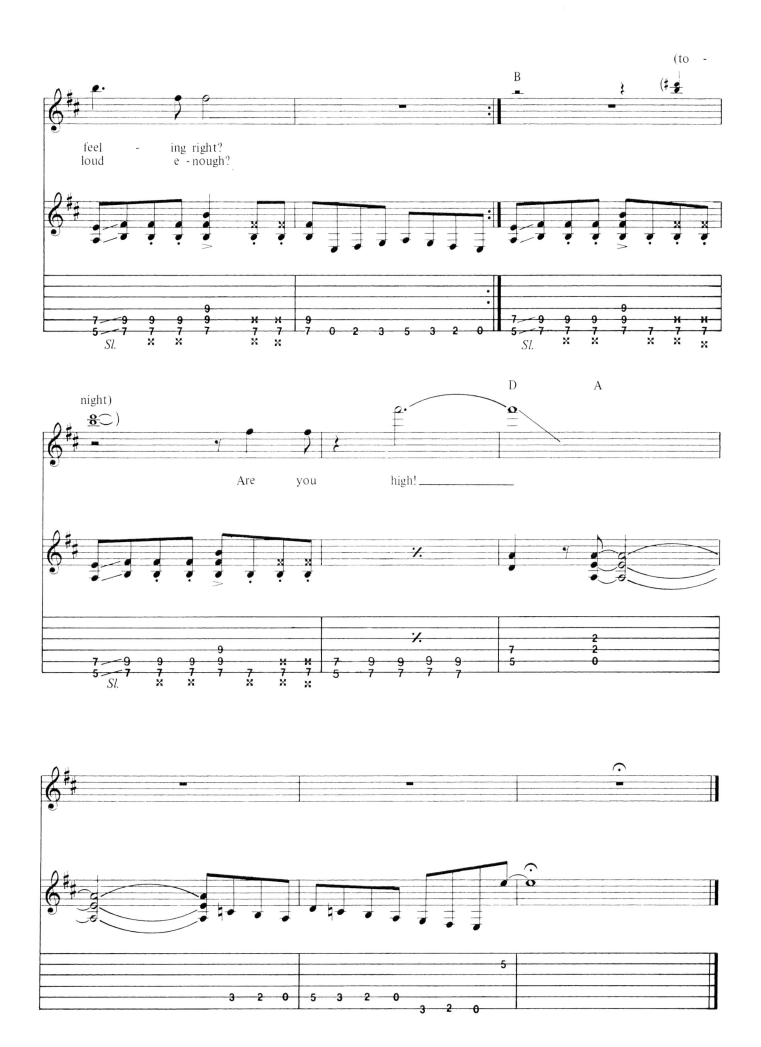

feel - ing right?
loud e - nough?

night)

Are you high!

Attack of the Mad Axeman

Words and Music by Michael Schenker and Gary Barden

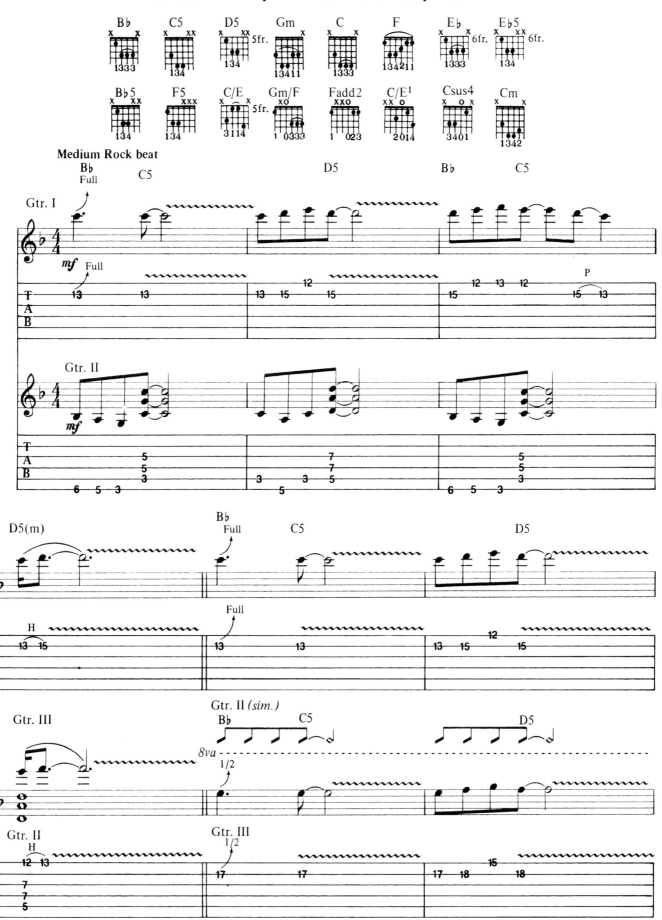

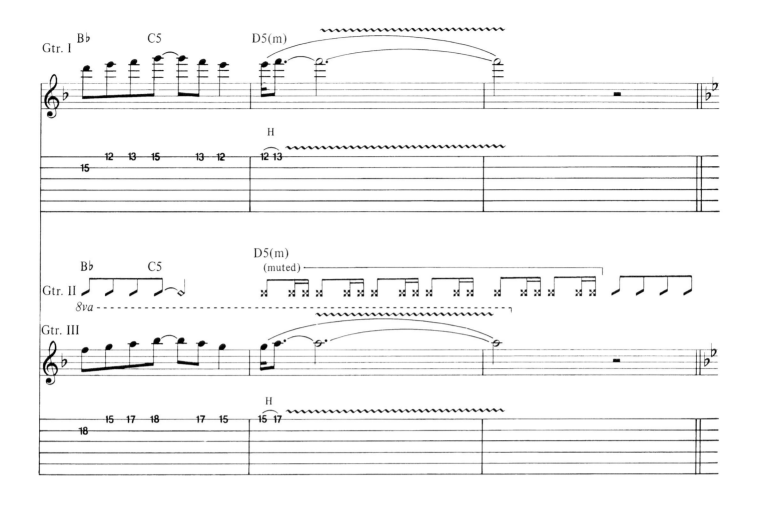

Sneak - in' 'round the back ___ streets. Don't stay out too late. ___
round ___ town his laugh - ter sounds deep in - to the night. ___ That

He's got some - thing he wants to give to you. He
flash of knife in the flick - er - ing light's for you. He

calls in his dreams ___ with his phan - tom screams. ___
knows when he's down ___ but he's got to have more 'cause he

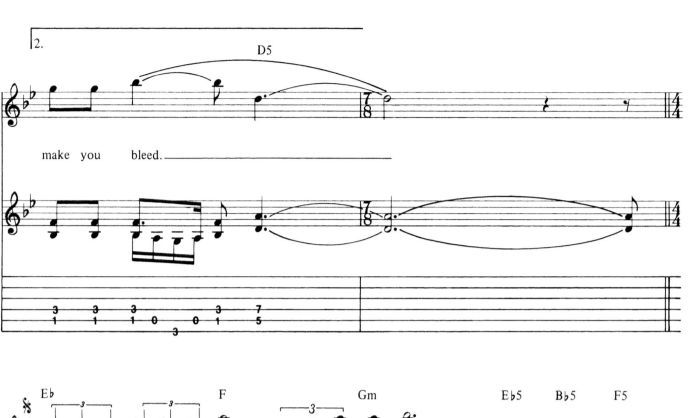

make you bleed.

Time af - ter time   you can   see him.
Time af - ter time in   the wings   you can   see him.

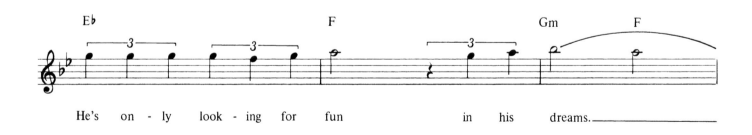

He's on - ly   look - ing   for   fun   in   his   dreams.

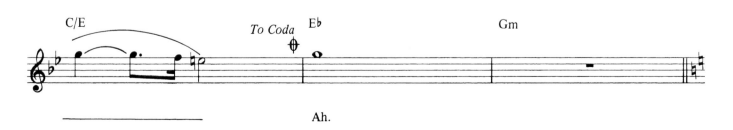

_____   Ah.

Interlude
Gtr. I *(Slide guitar solo)*

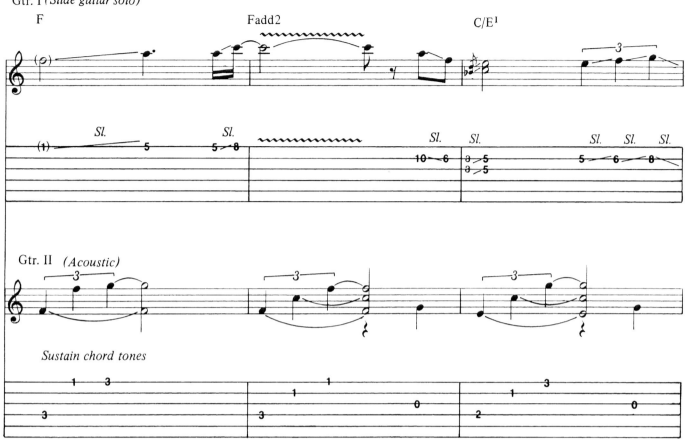

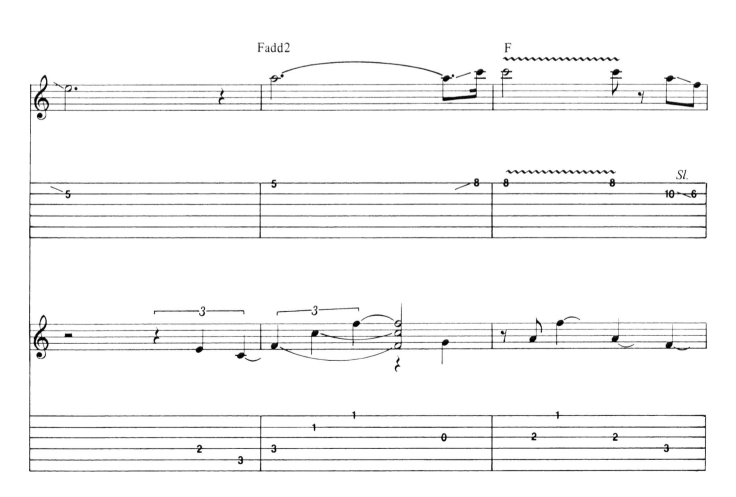

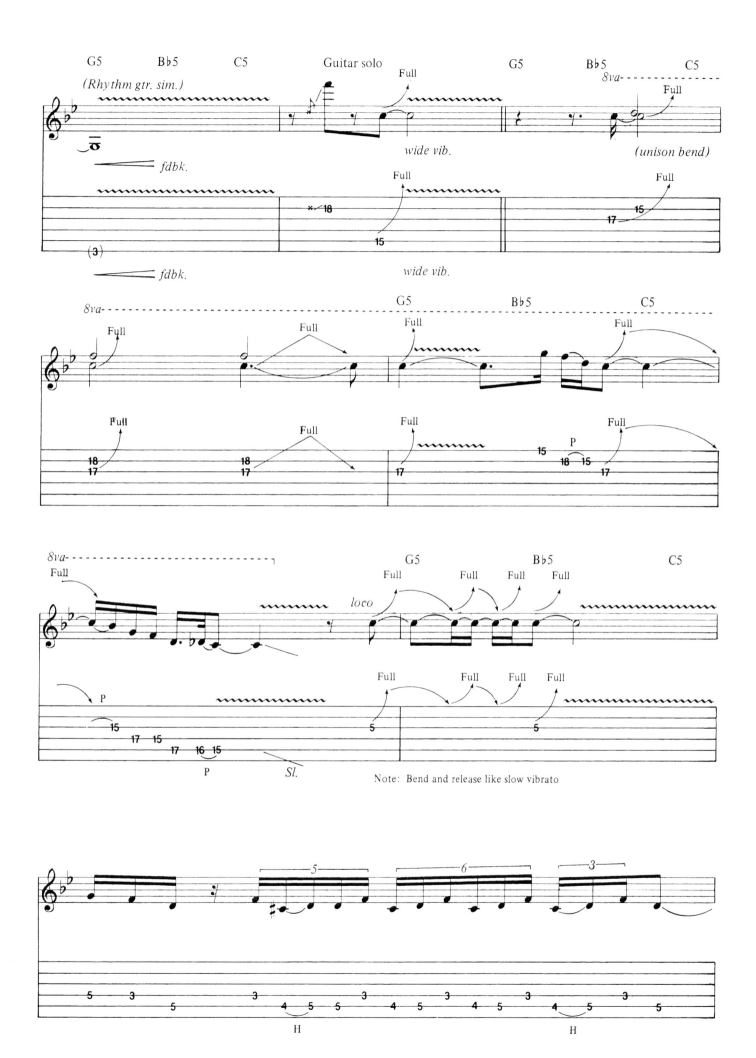

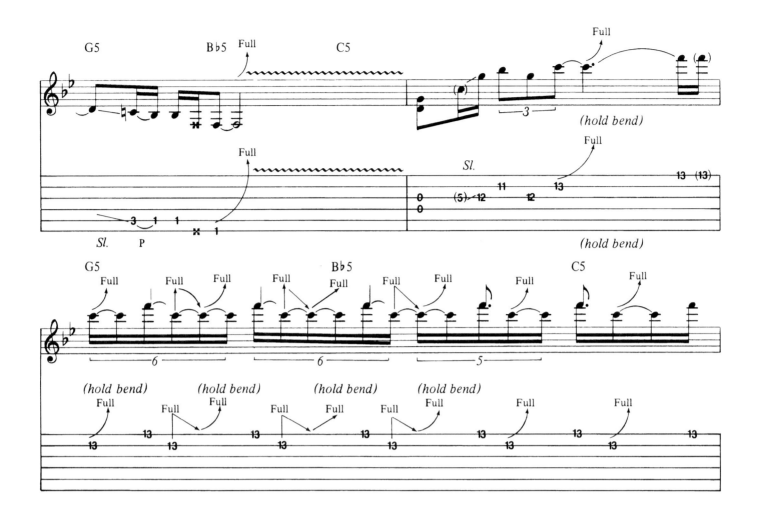

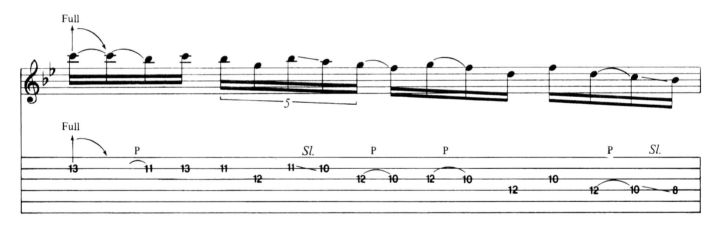

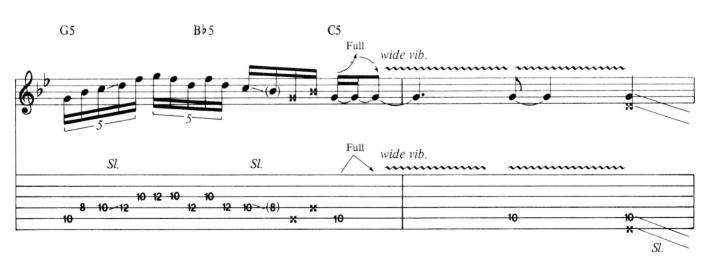

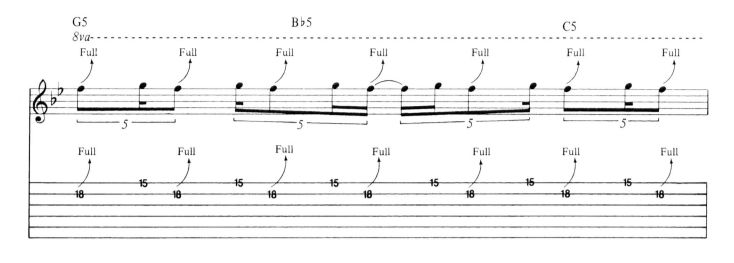

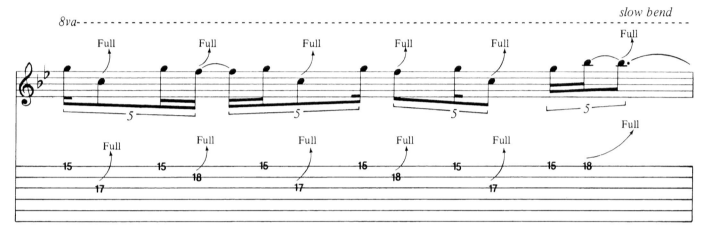

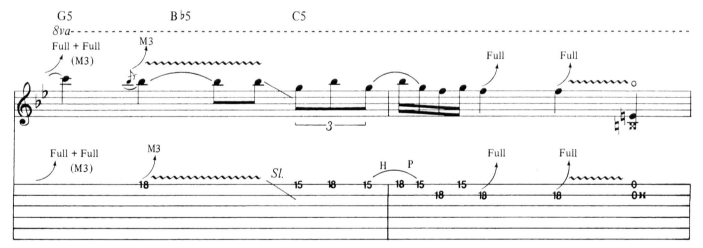

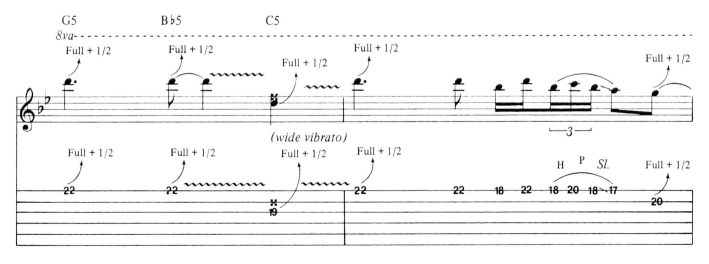

Captain Nemo

By Michael Schenker

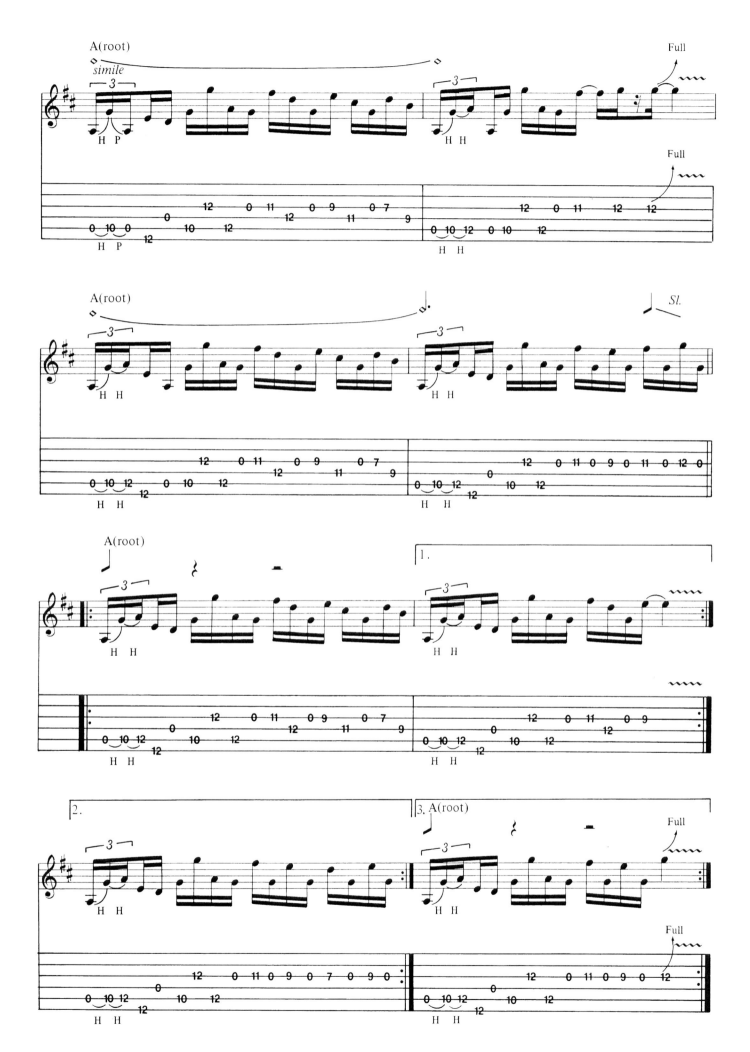

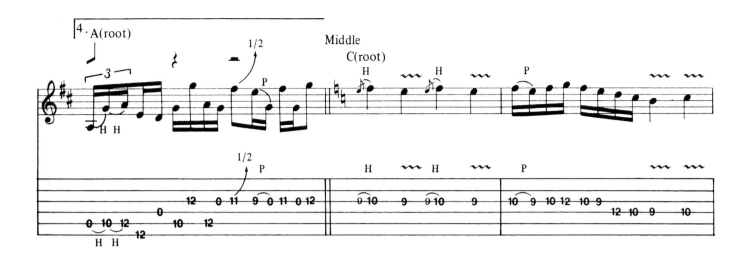

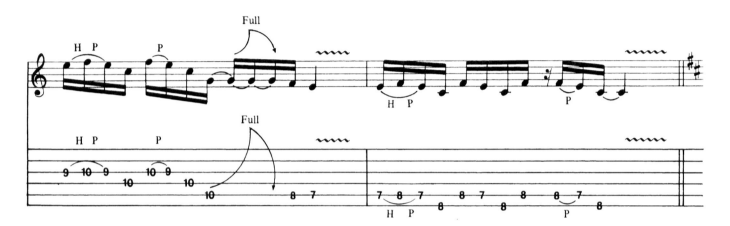

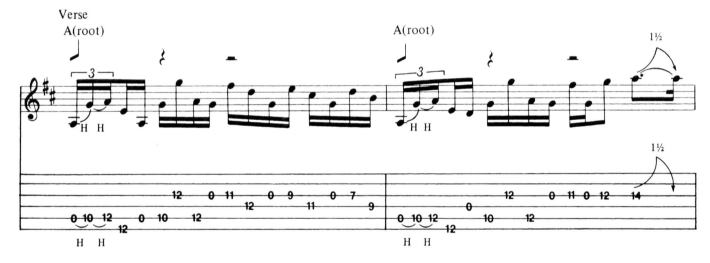

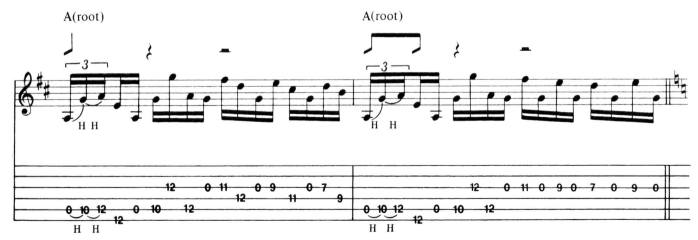

Middle 2

Verse

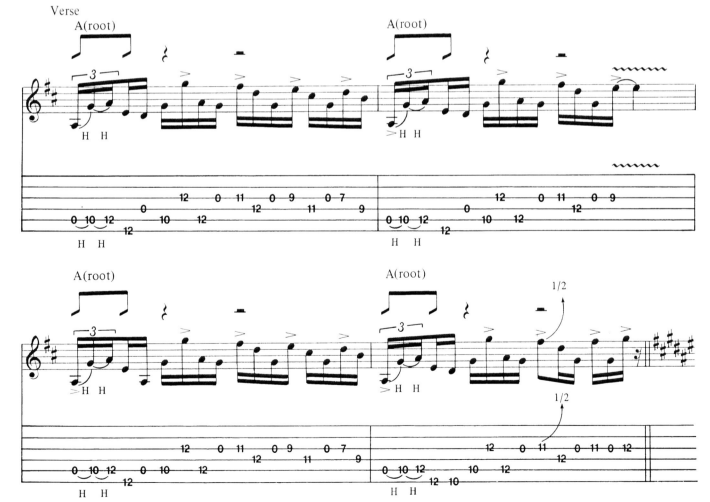

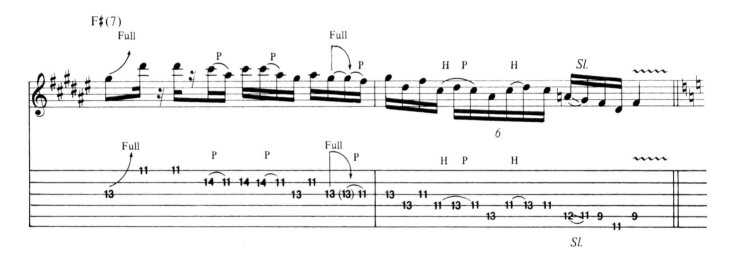

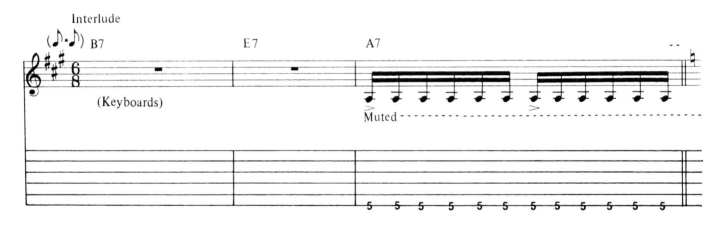

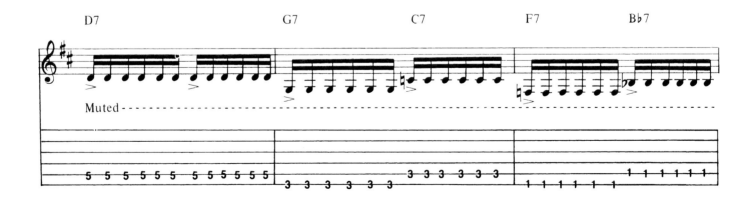

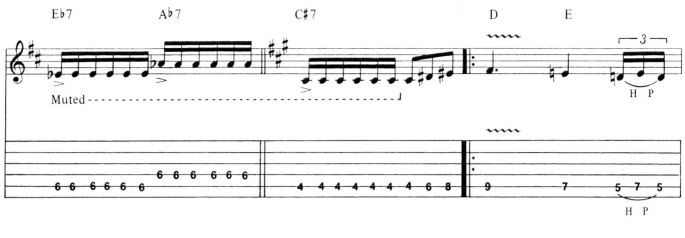

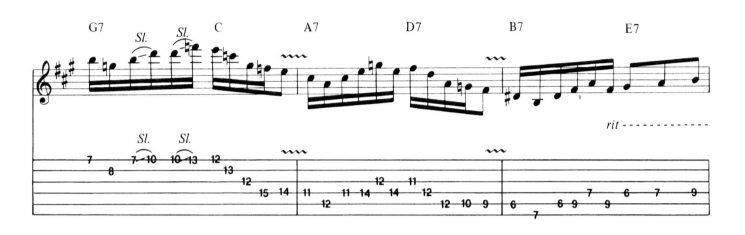

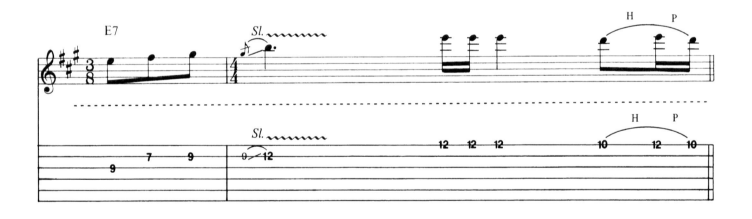

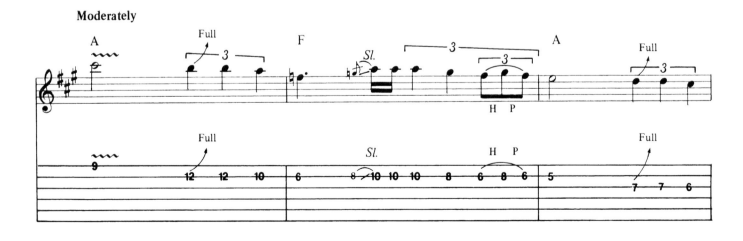

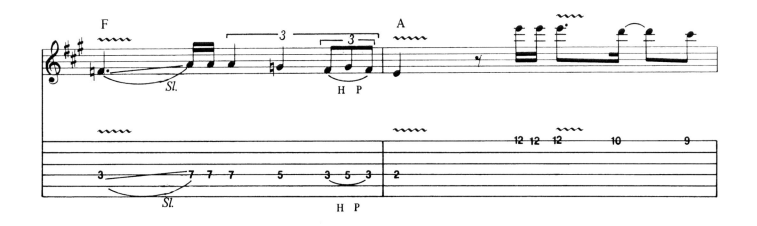

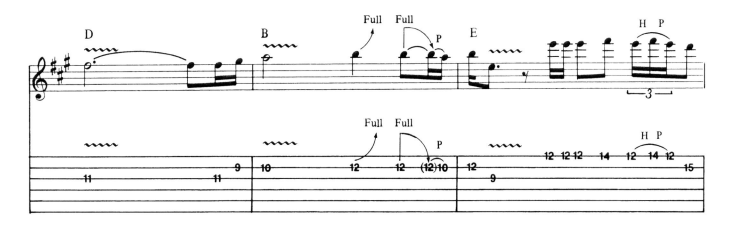

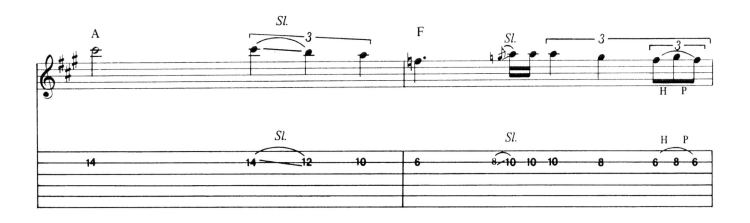

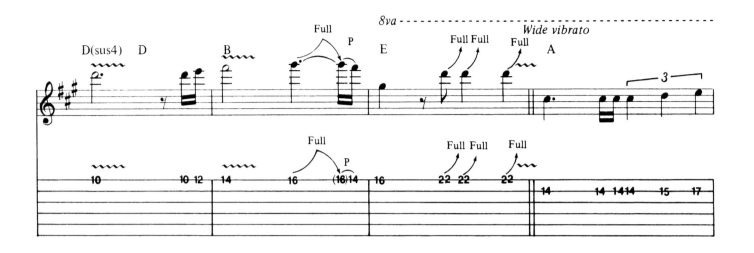

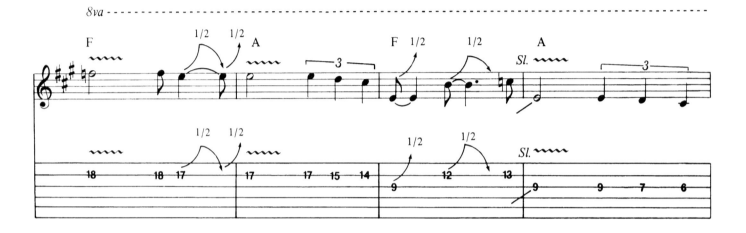

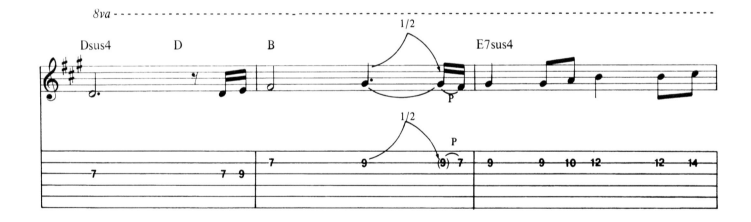

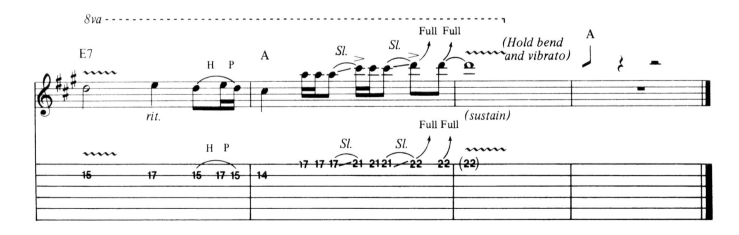

Cry for the Nations

Words and Music by Michael Schenker and Gary Barden

Note: Keyboard intro adapted for guitar—use clean tone with octave divider to simulate synth. tone.

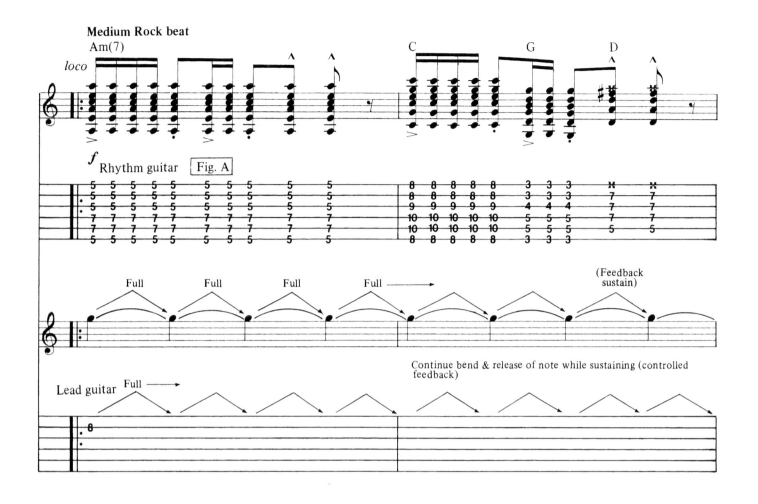

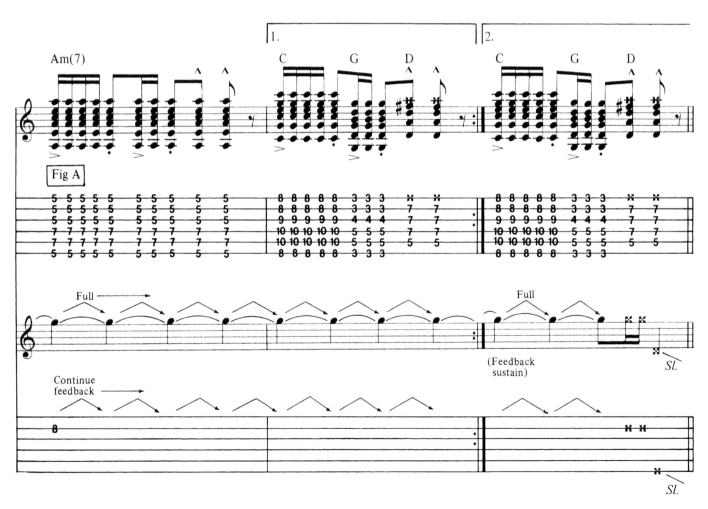

Verse

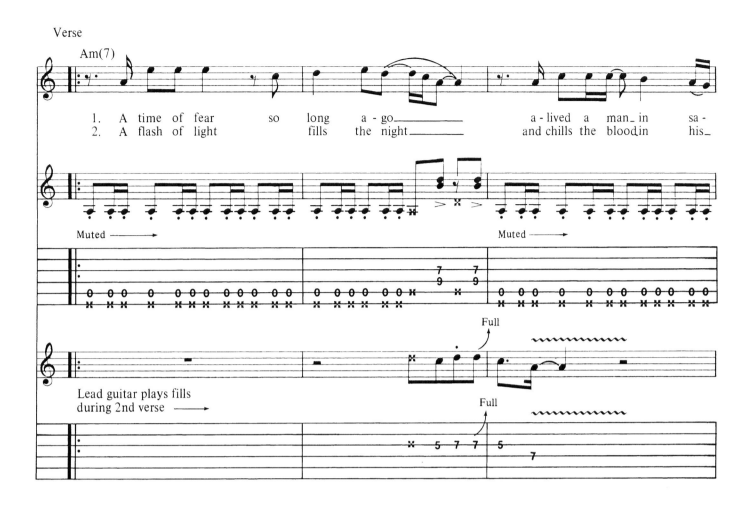

1. A time of fear so long a - go_____ a - lived a man_ in sa -
2. A flash of light fills the night_____ and chills the blood in his_

Muted ⟶   Muted ⟶

Lead guitar plays fills
during 2nd verse ⟶

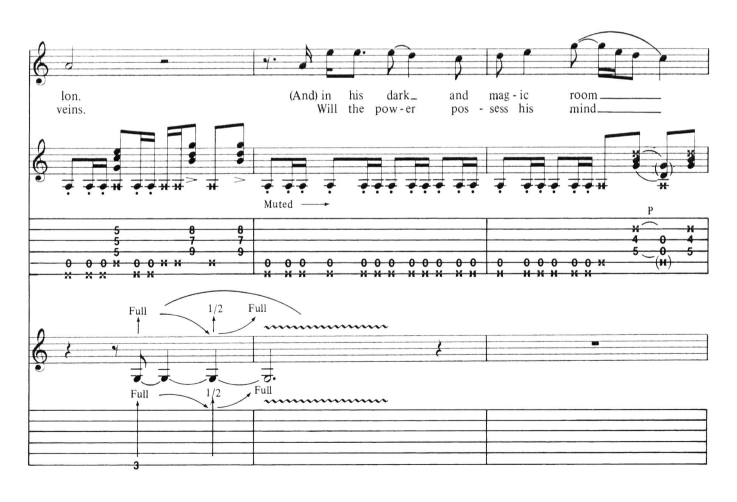

lon.   (And) in his dark_ and mag - ic room_____
veins.   Will the pow - er pos - sess his mind_____

Muted ⟶

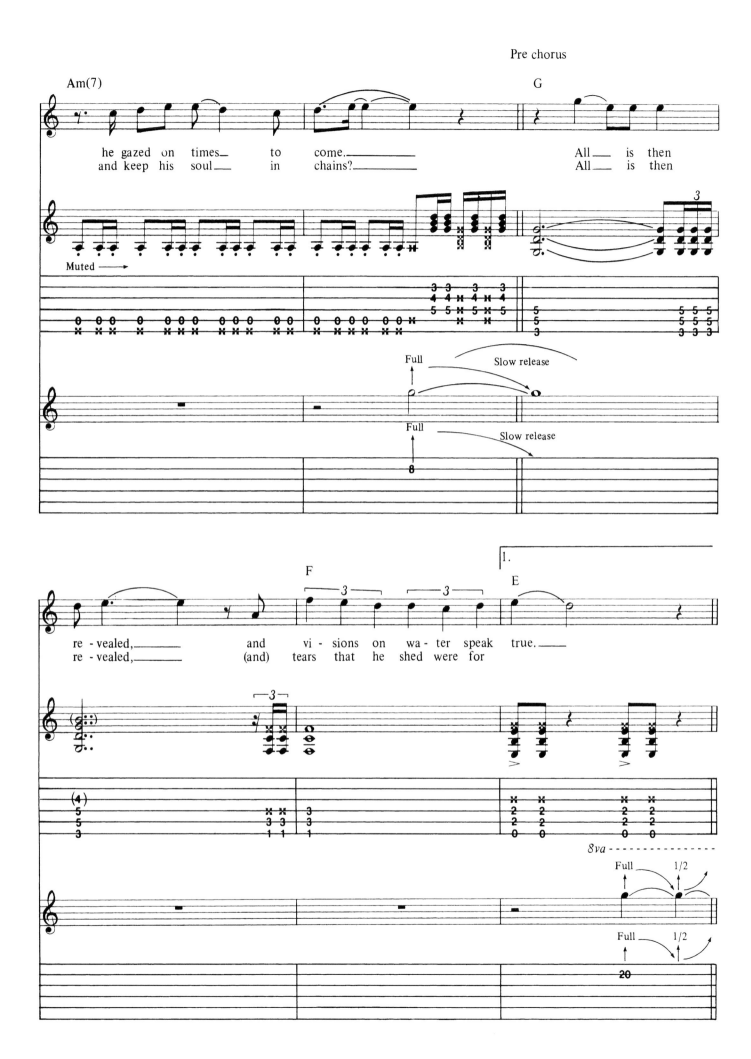

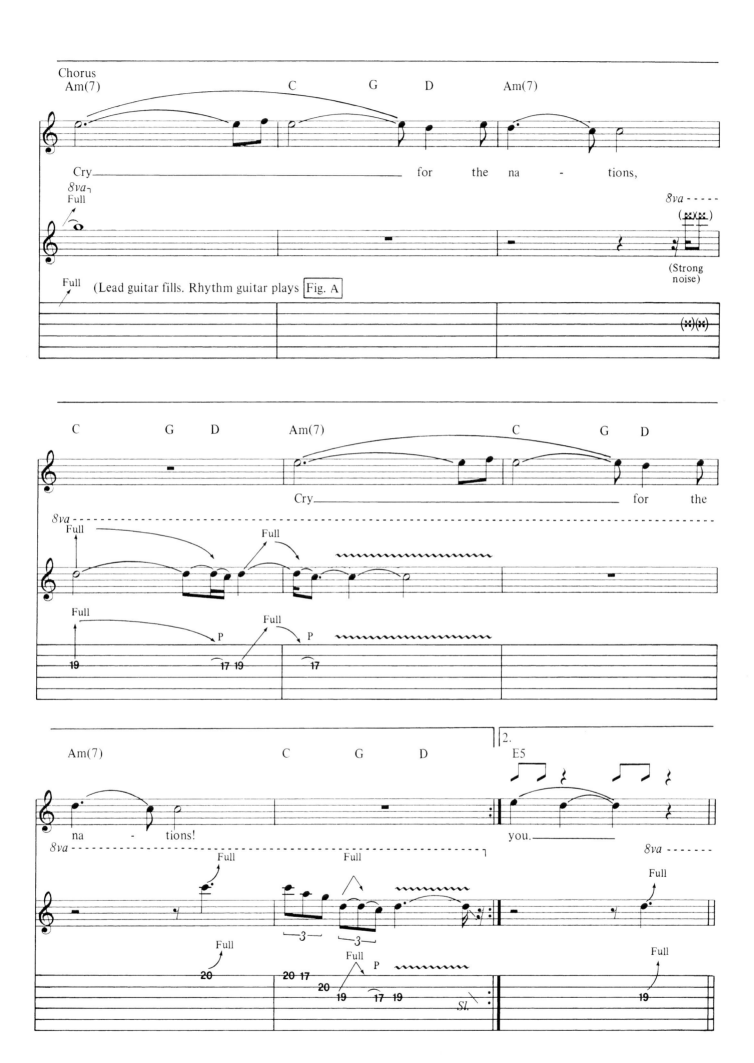

Chorus No. 2

Rhythm guitar continues Fig. A

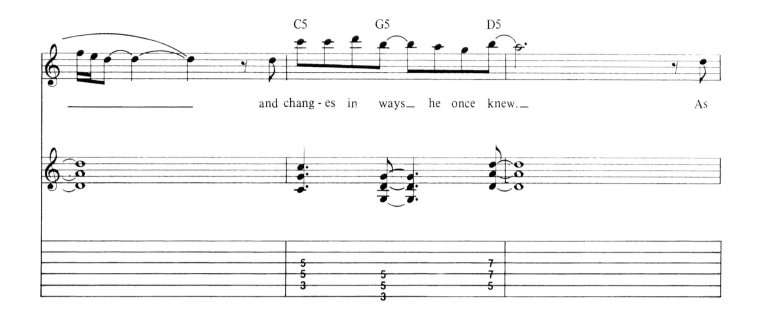

and chang - es in ways_ he once knew._ As

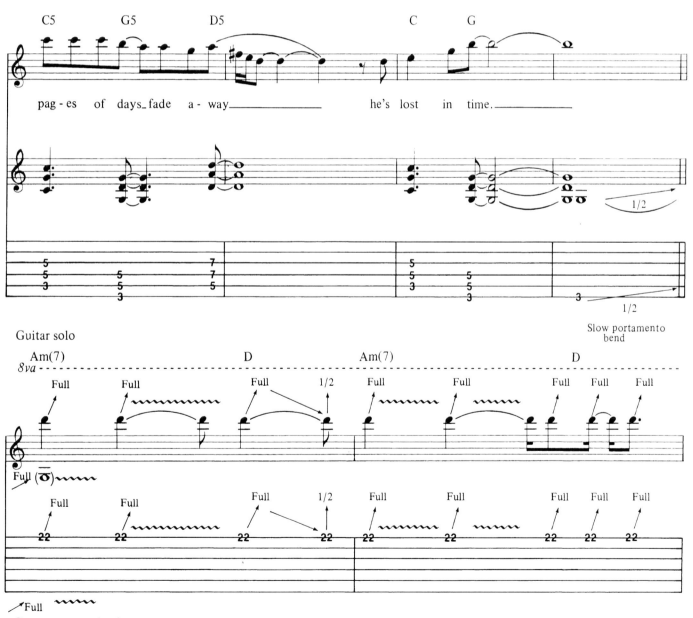

pag - es of days_ fade a - way_____ he's lost in time._____

Slow portamento bend

Guitar solo

Slow portamento bend

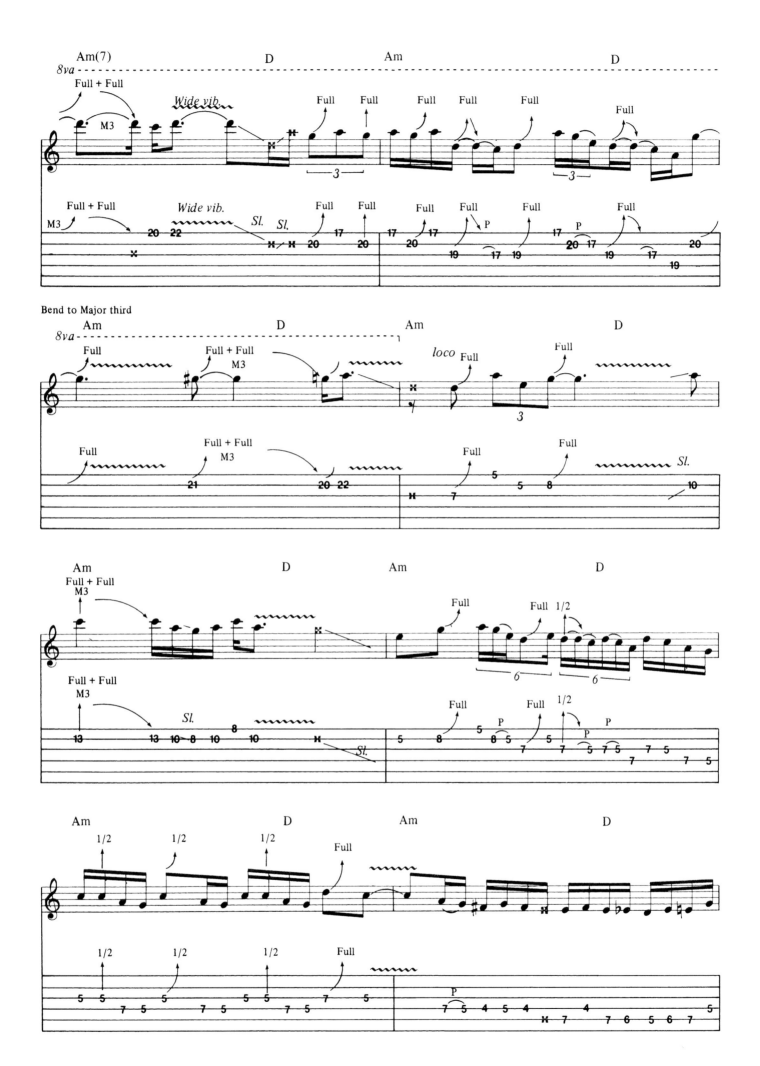

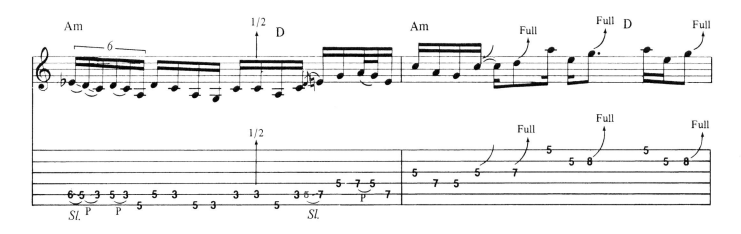

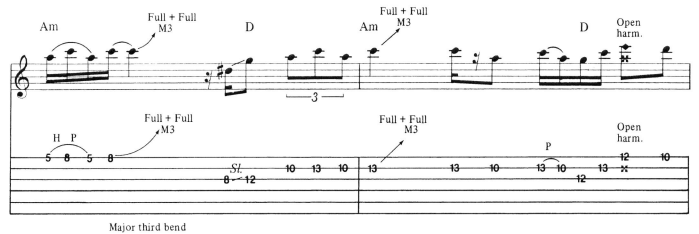

Major third bend

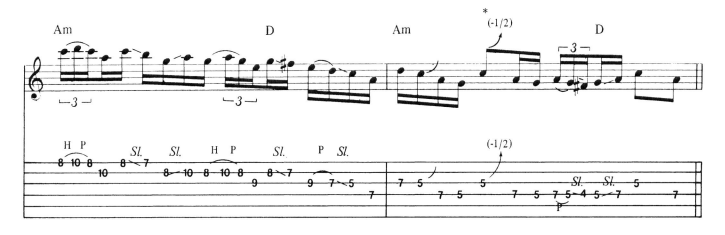

* Note: Slightly less than a semitone bend.

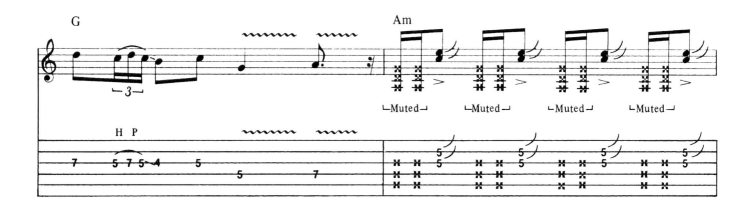

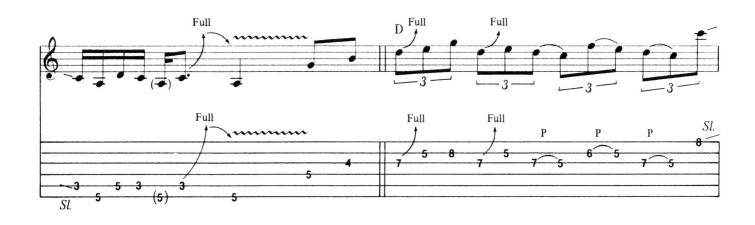

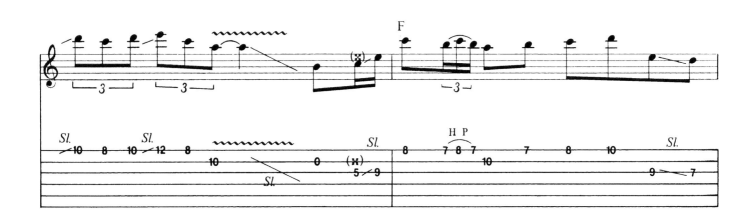

Instrumental Bridge (add vocal effects: high screams, etc.)

"Outro" (Outchorus)

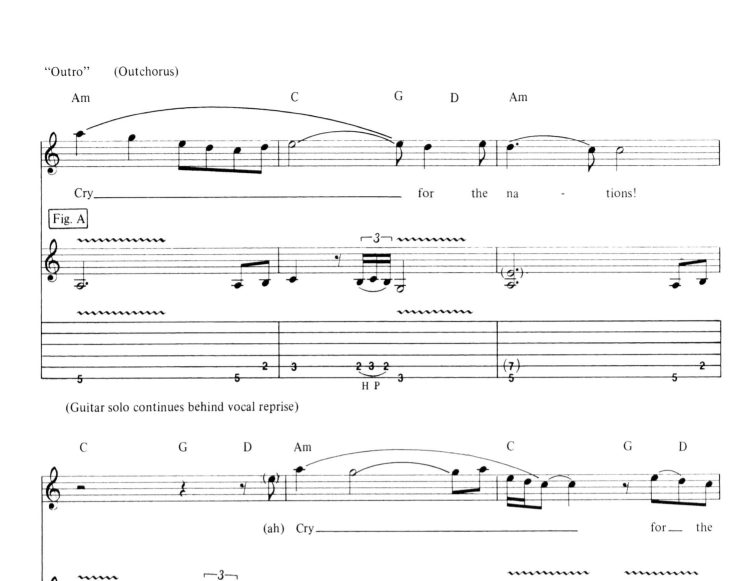

(Guitar solo continues behind vocal reprise)

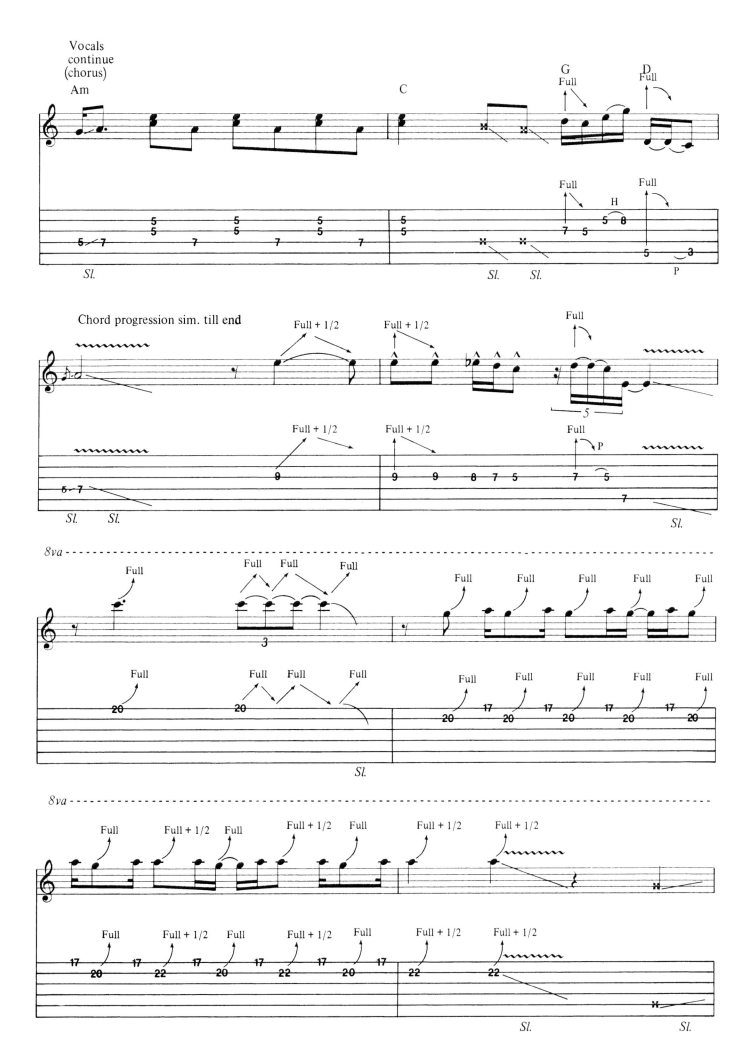

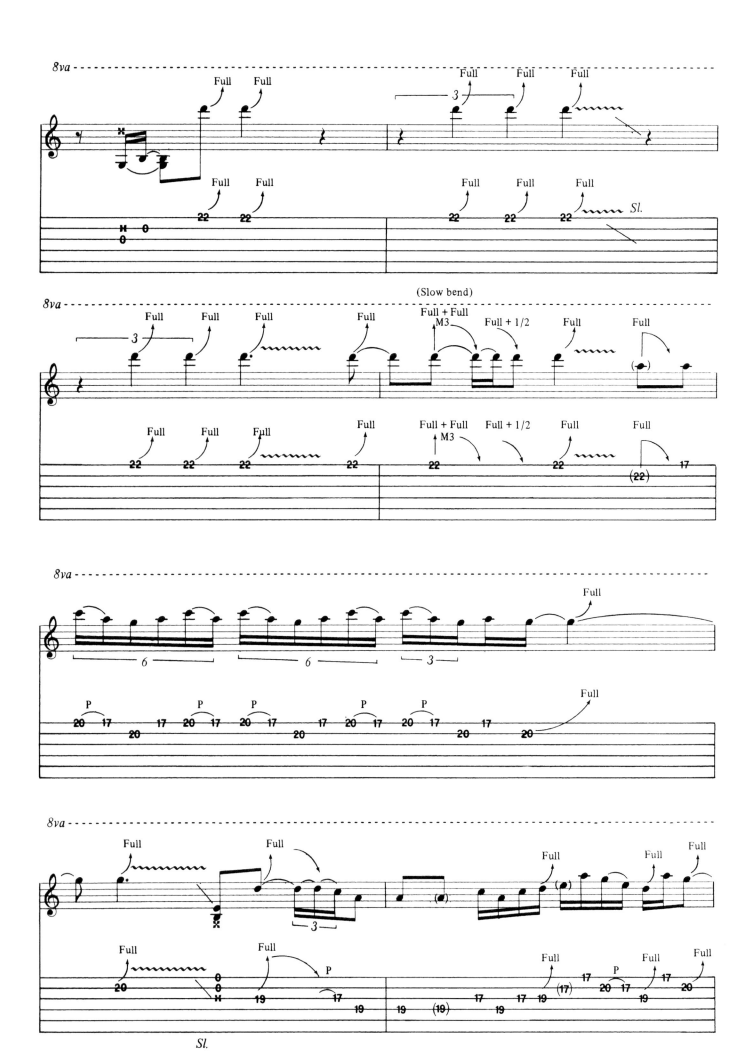

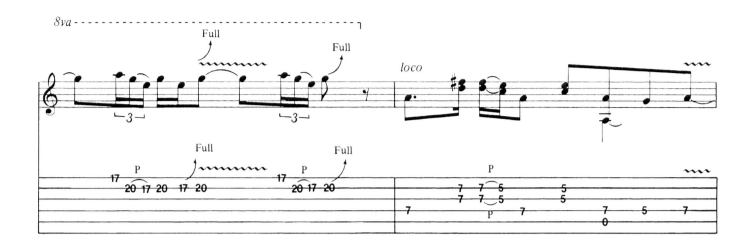

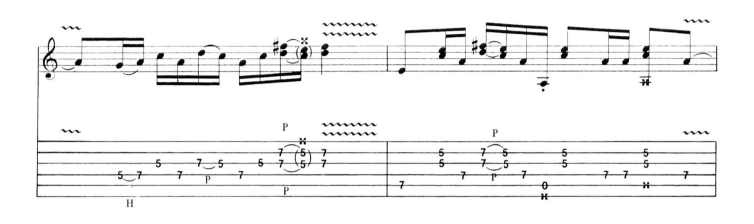

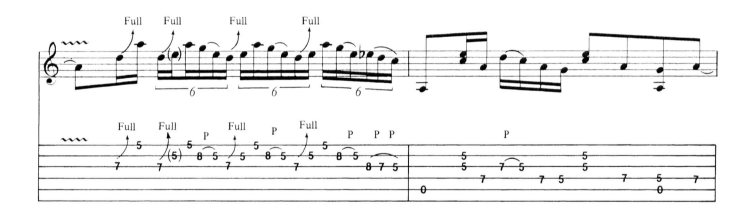

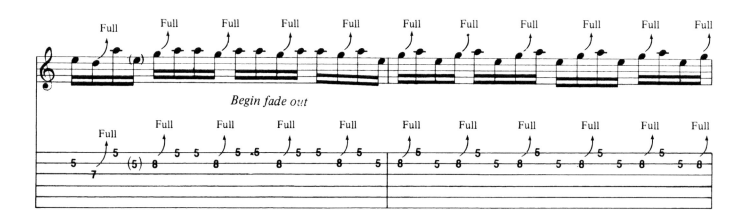

Begin fade out

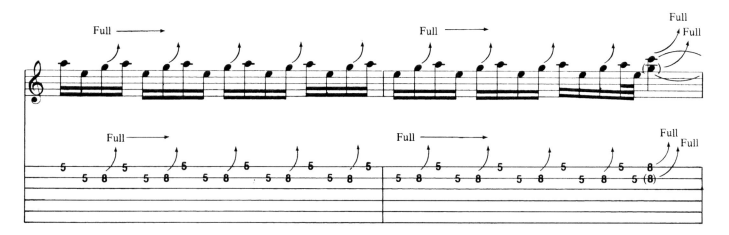

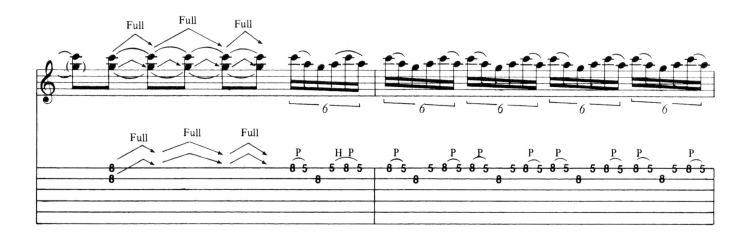

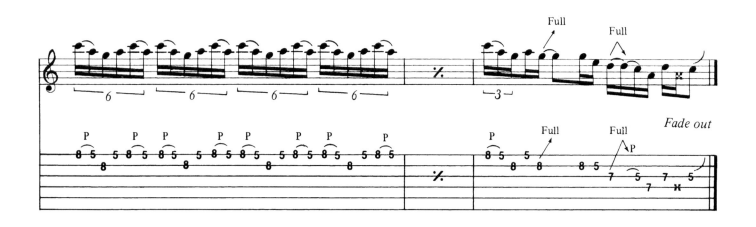

Fade out

Doctor, Doctor

Words and Music by Phillip John Mogg and Michael Schenker

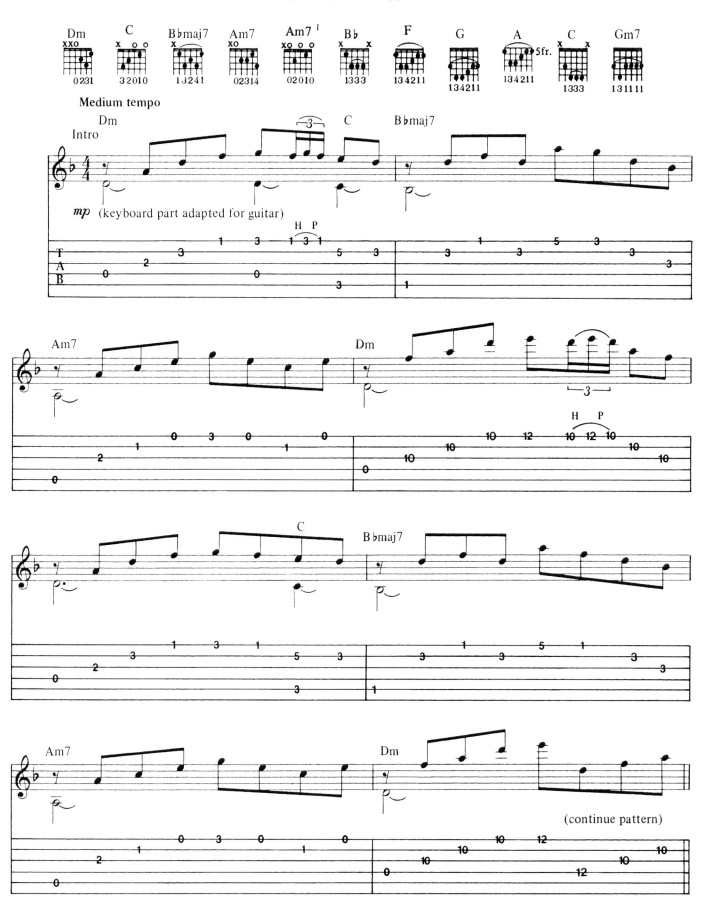

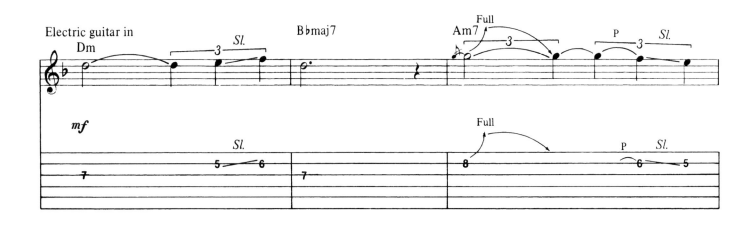

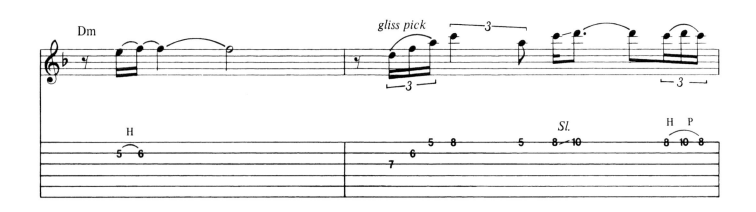

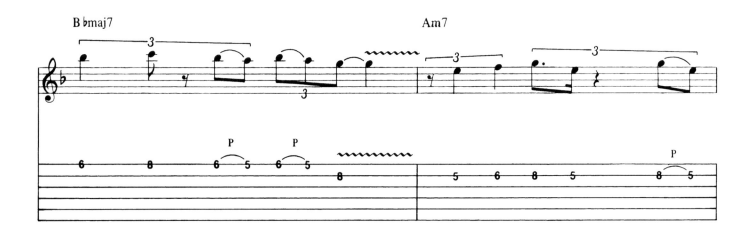

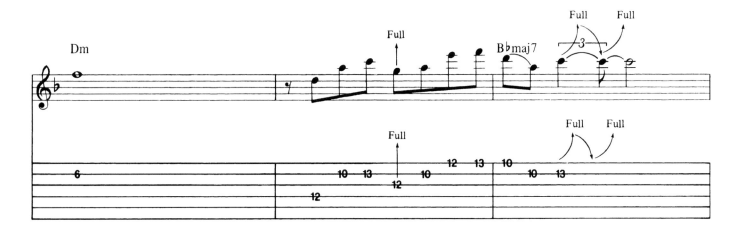

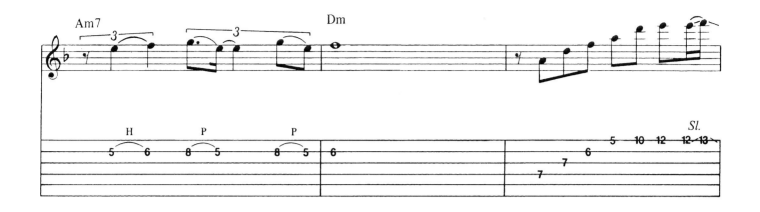

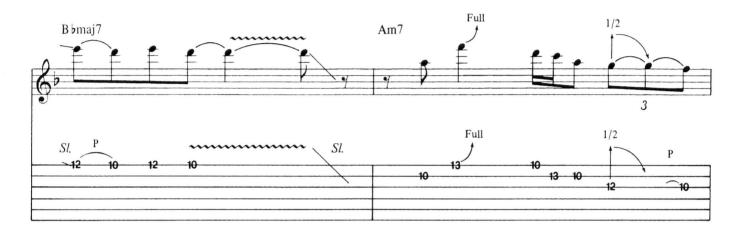

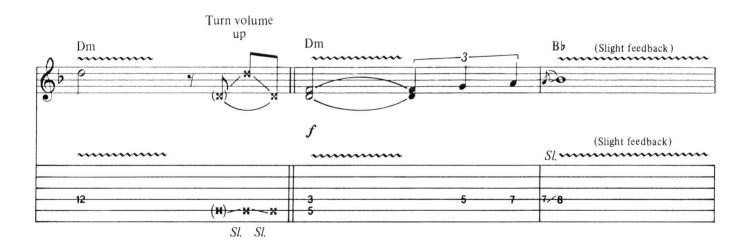

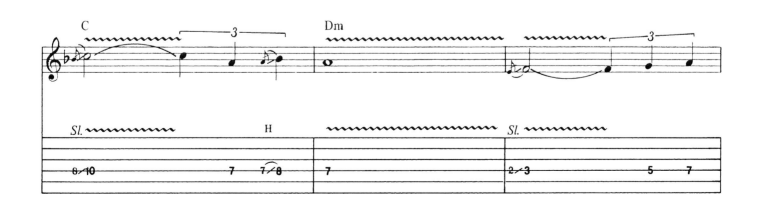

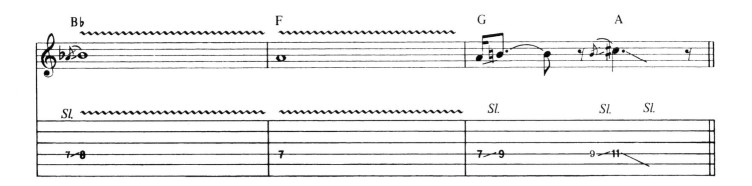

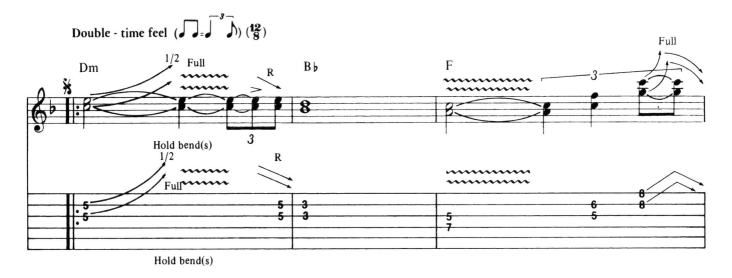

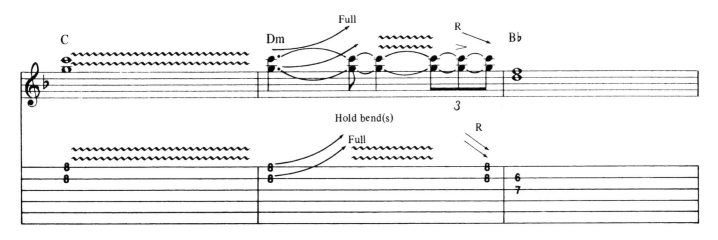

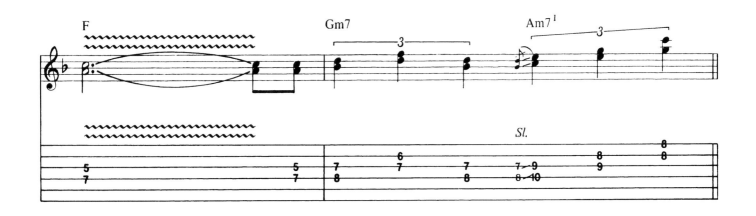

62

Liv - in', lov - in', I'm on the run so___ far a - way___ from

64

Gimme Your Love

Words and Music by Robin McAuley and Rocky Newton

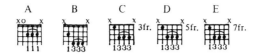

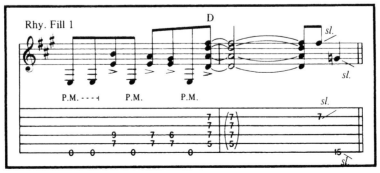

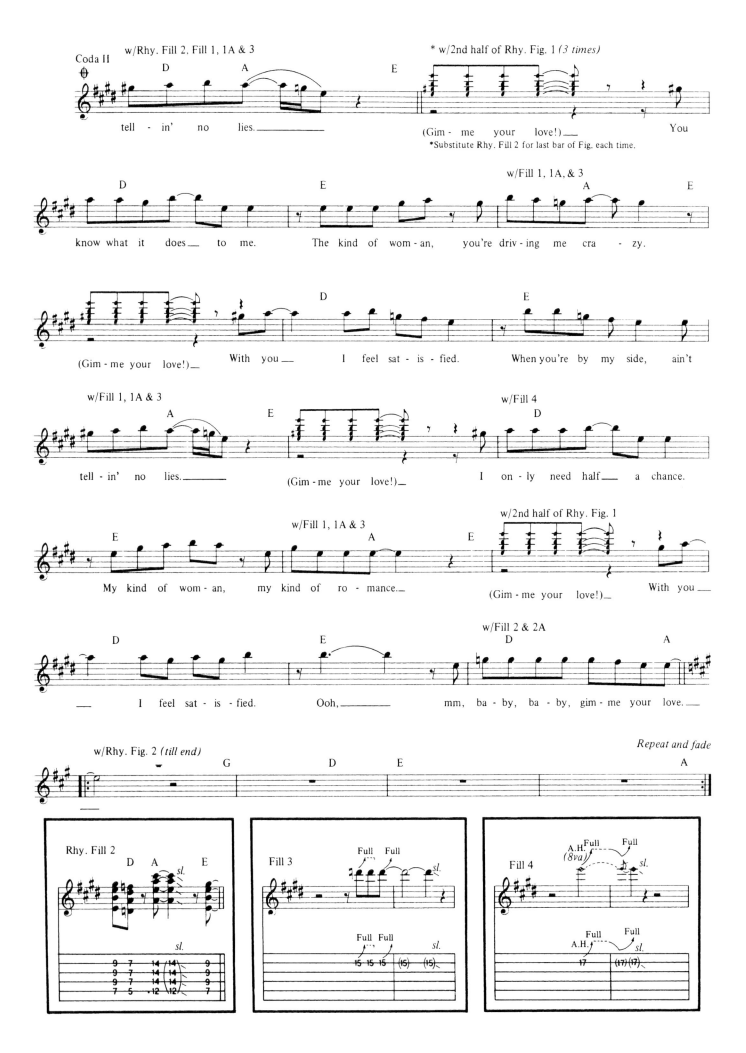

Into the Arena

By Michael Schenker

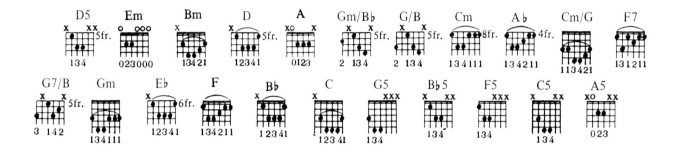

Moderately fast Rock beat

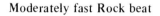

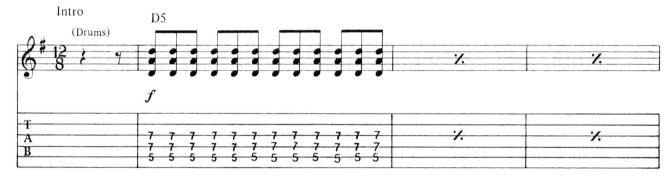

Main theme
Note: (Add wah-wah pedal filtering to theme)
on repeat: muted

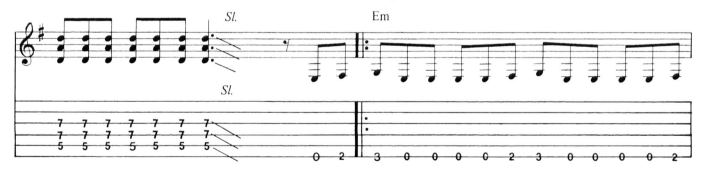

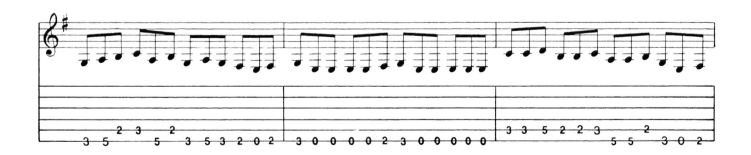

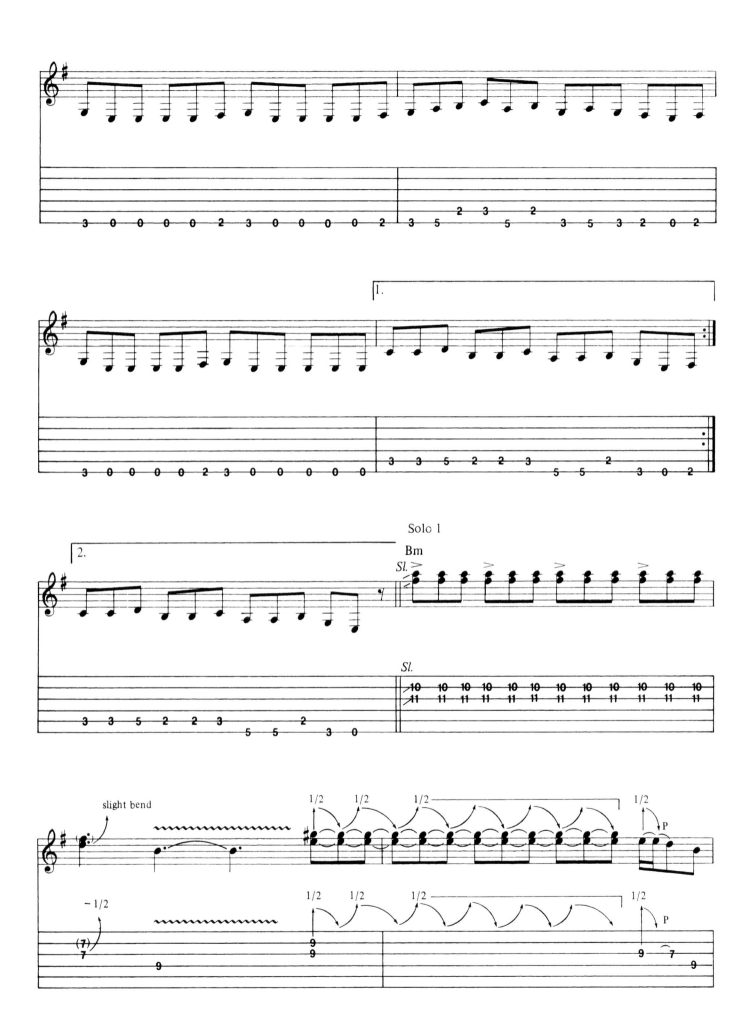

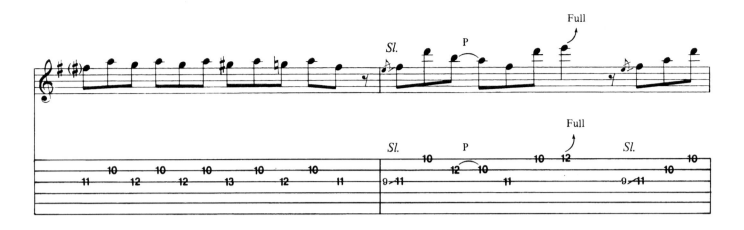

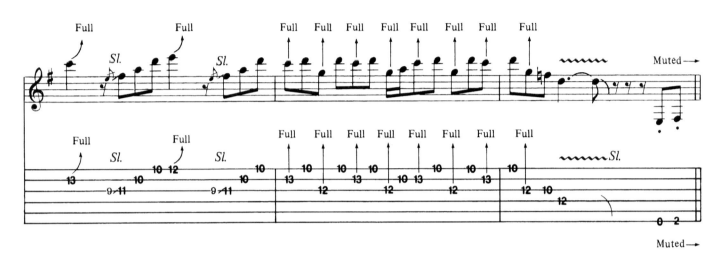

Em

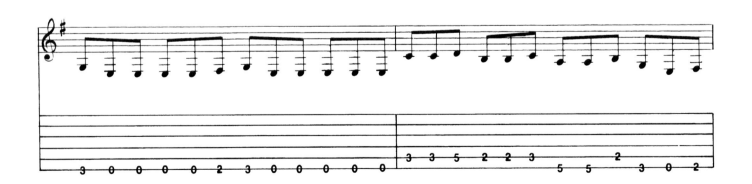

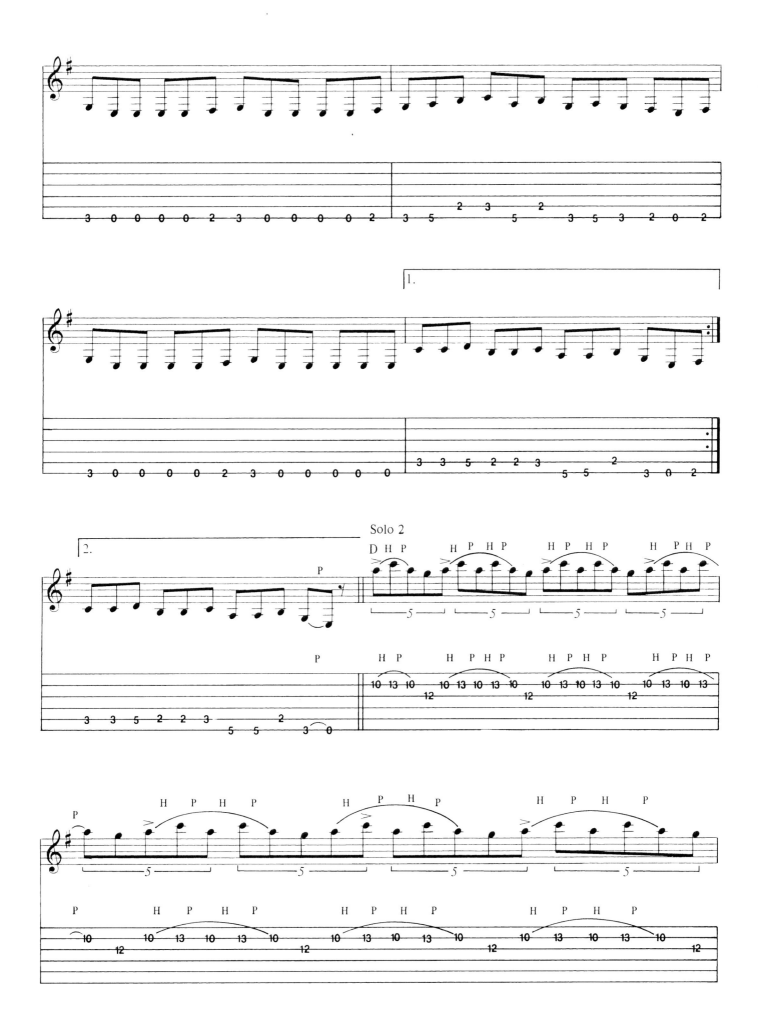

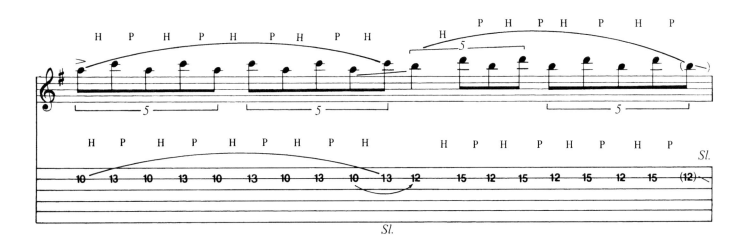

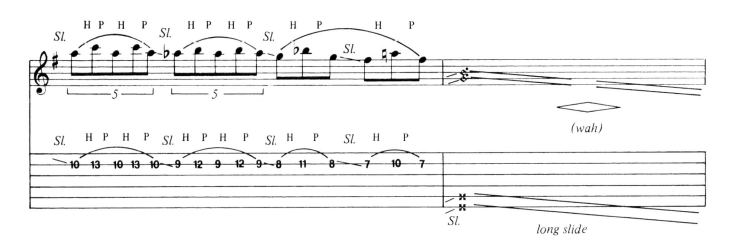

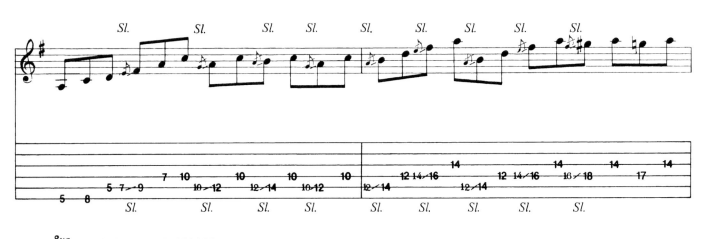

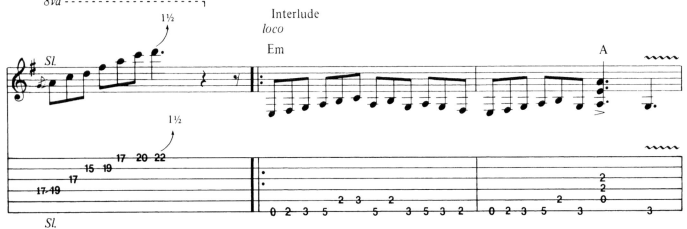

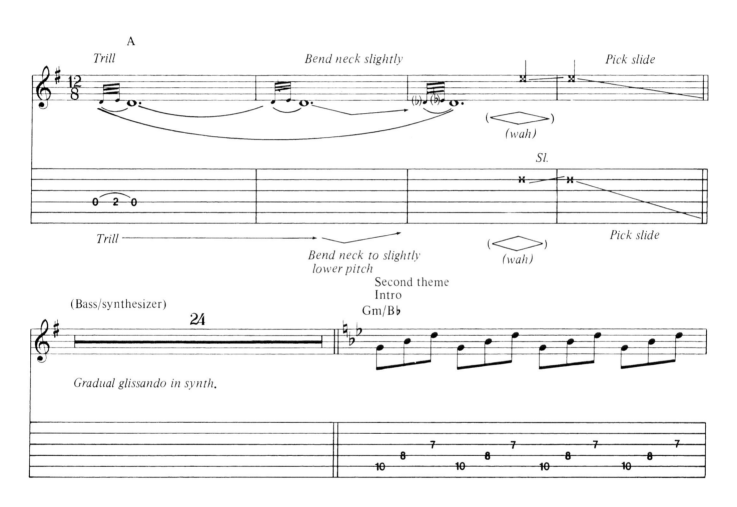

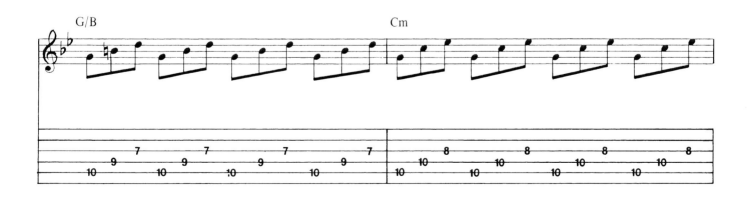

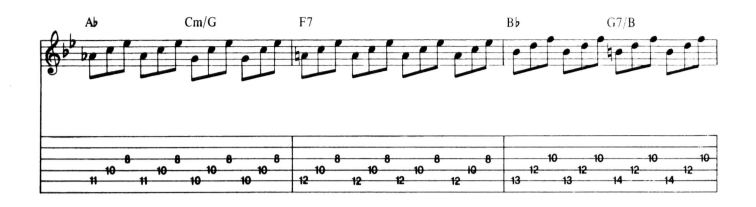

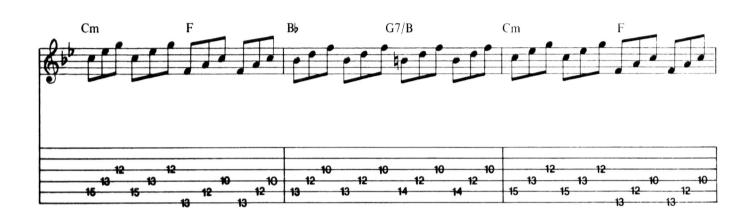

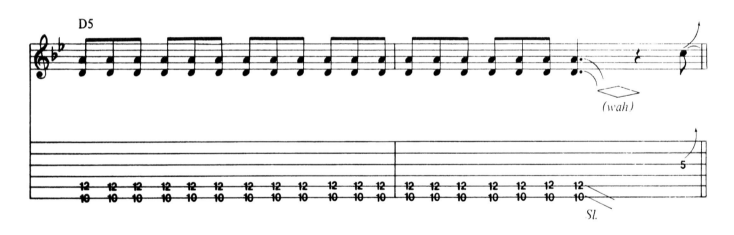

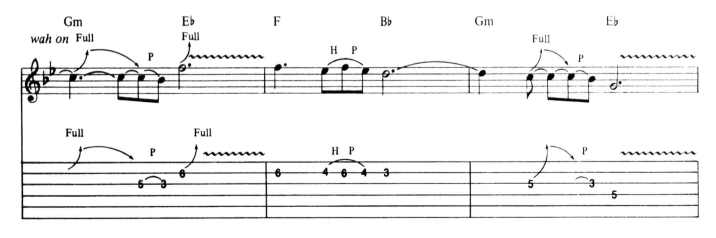

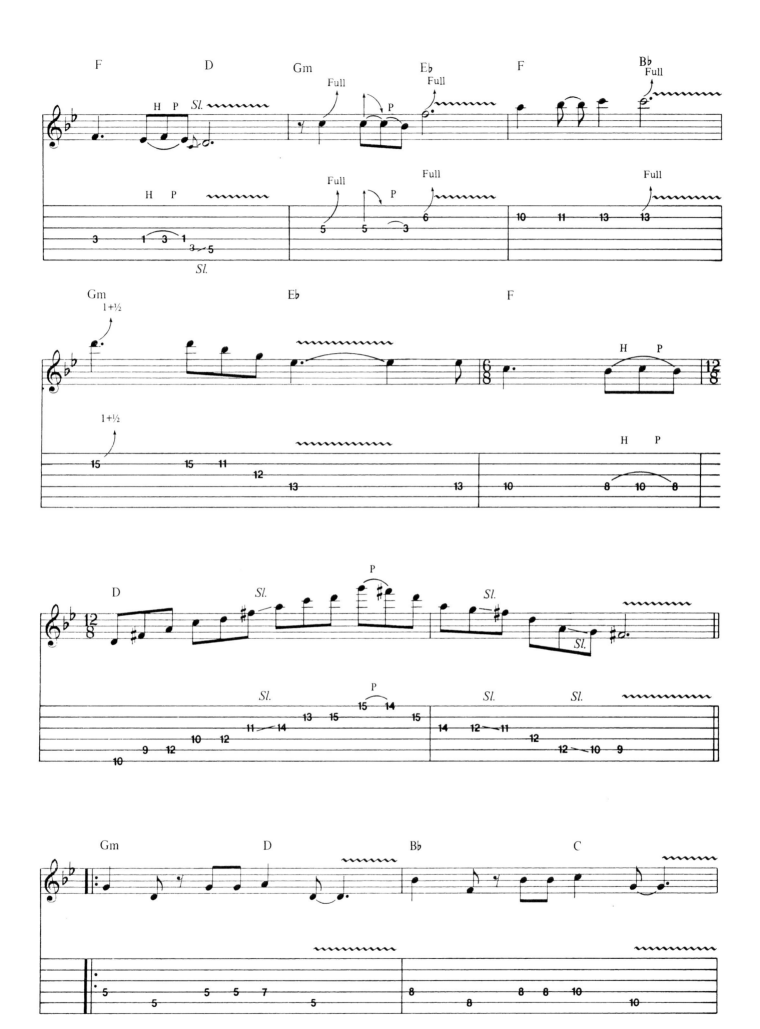

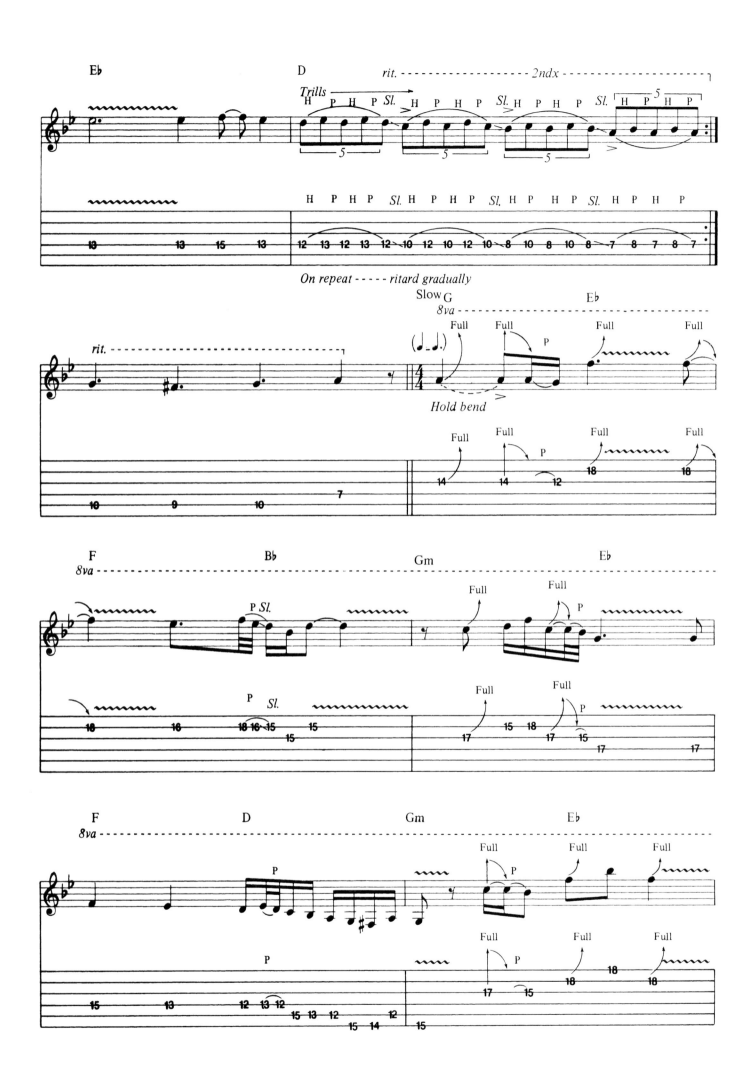

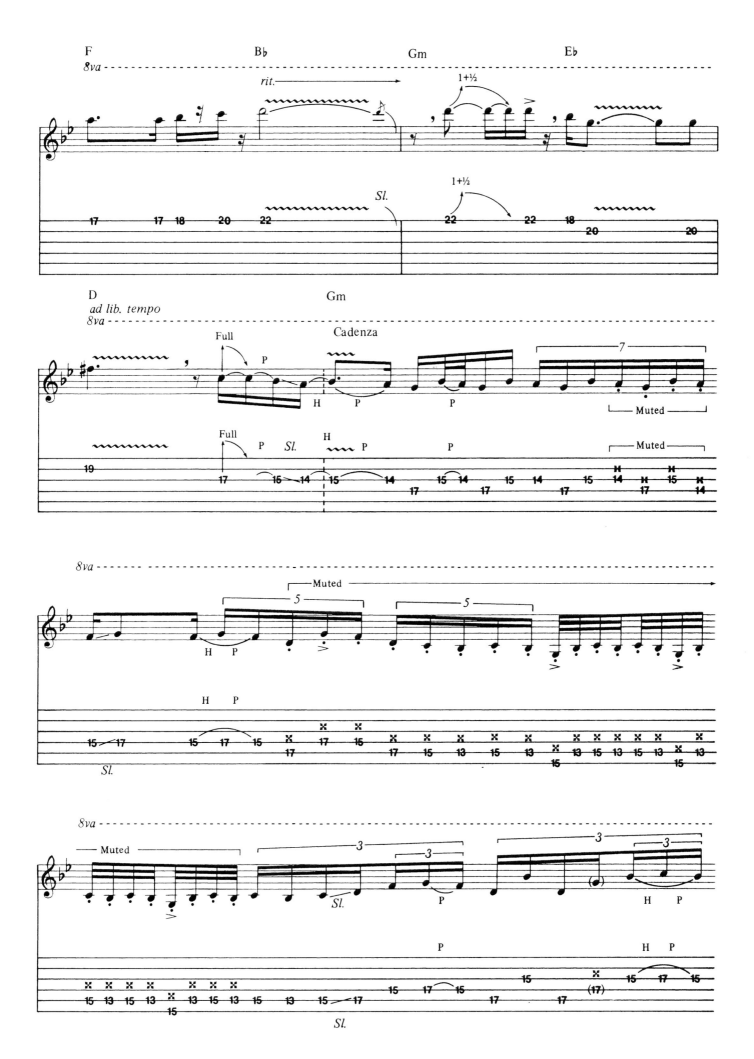

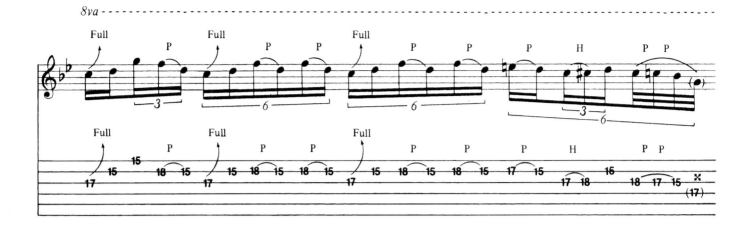

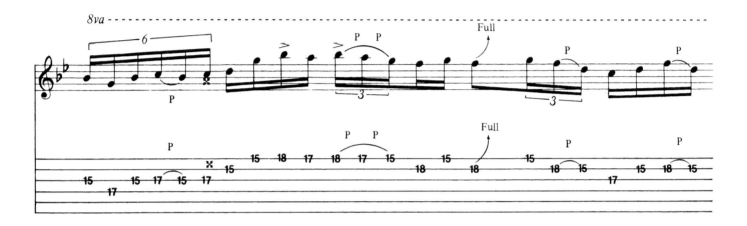

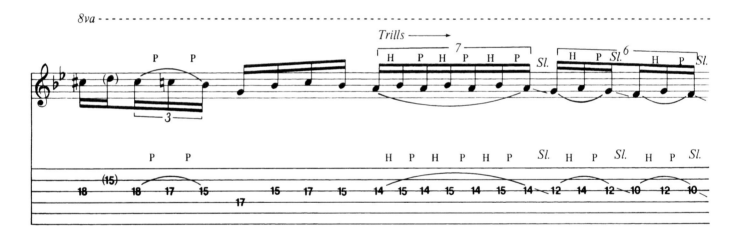

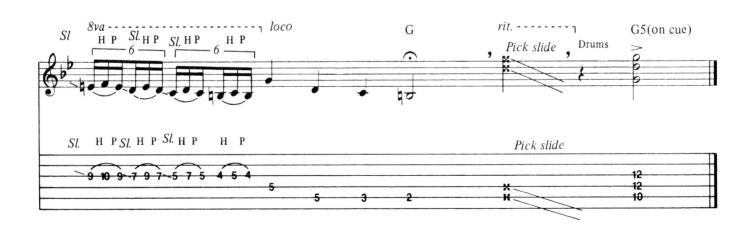

Lights Out

Words and Music by Michael Schenker, Phil Mogg, Andy Parker and Pete Way

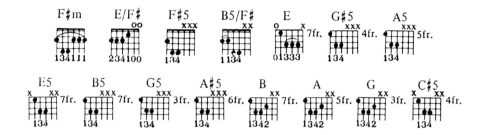

Verse

1. When love's back and the bat - tle's charg - ing, ___ runs all the way. ___

Up to the front, I'm ___ not go - in'.

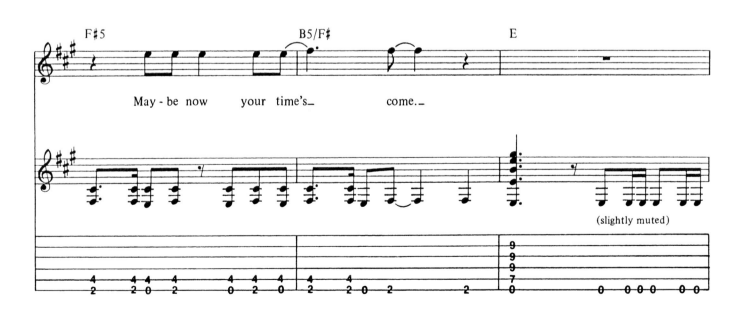

May - be now your time's ___ come. ___

(slightly muted)

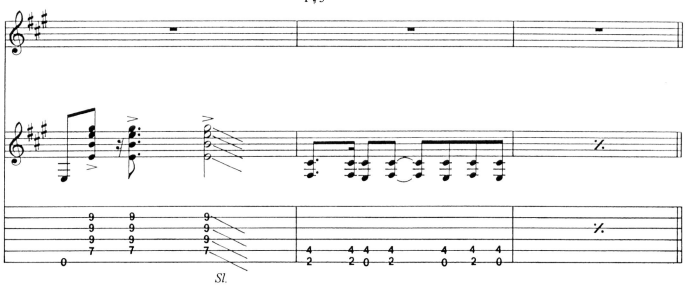

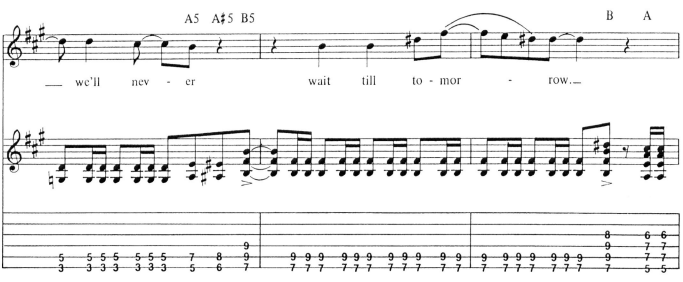

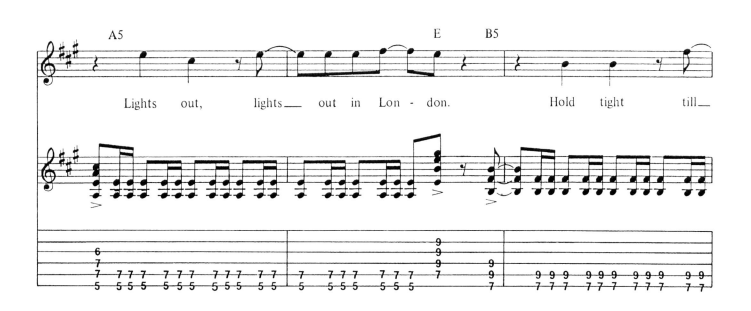

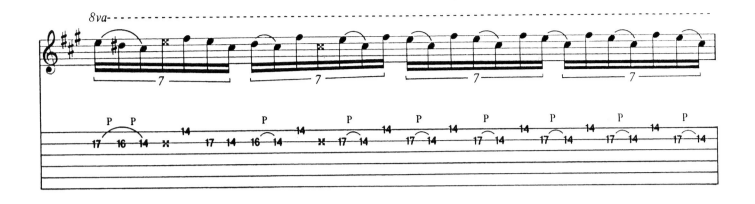

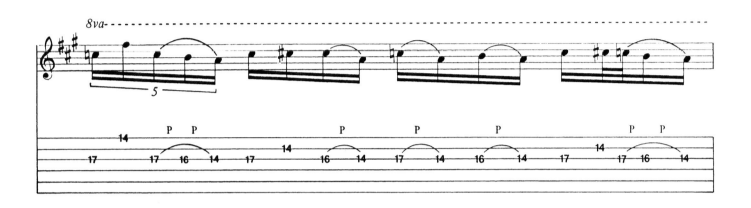

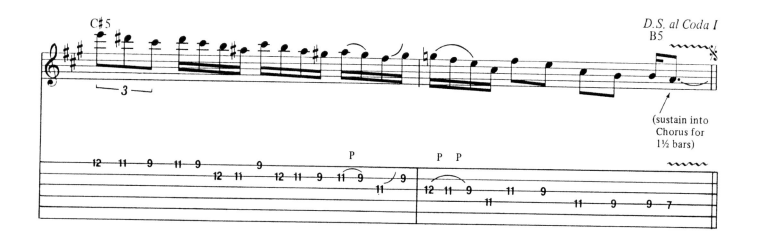

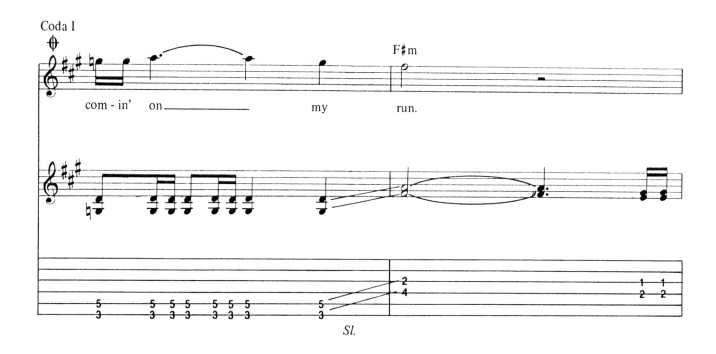

com - in' on_____ my run.

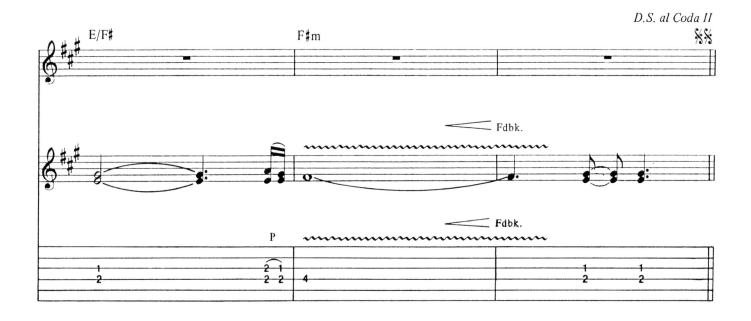

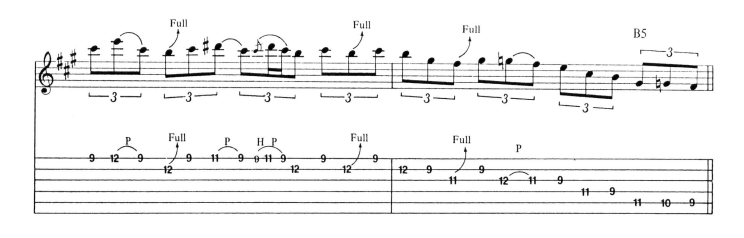

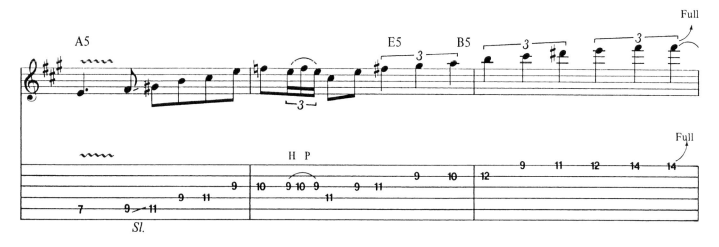

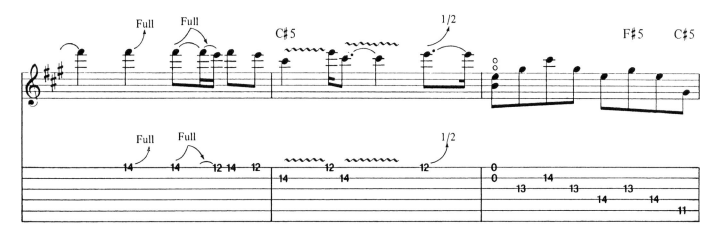

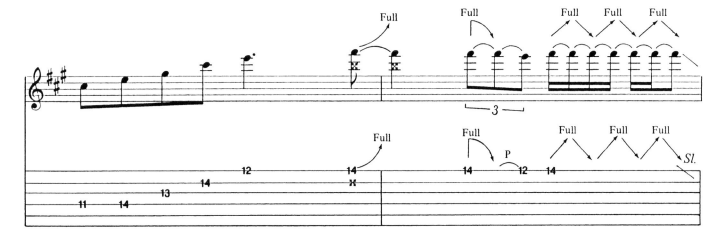

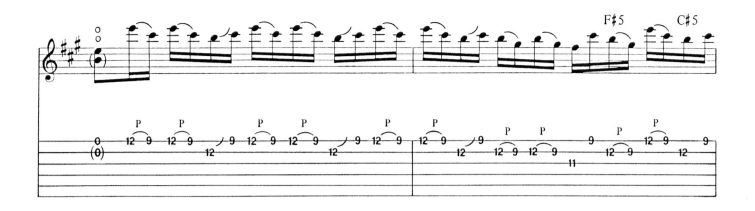

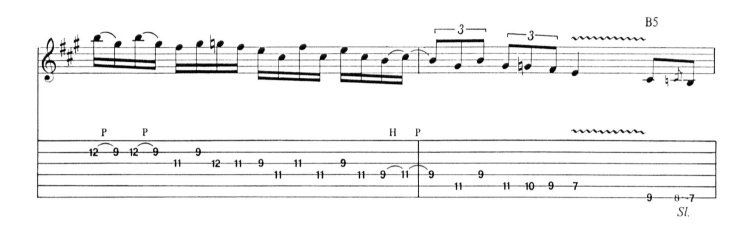

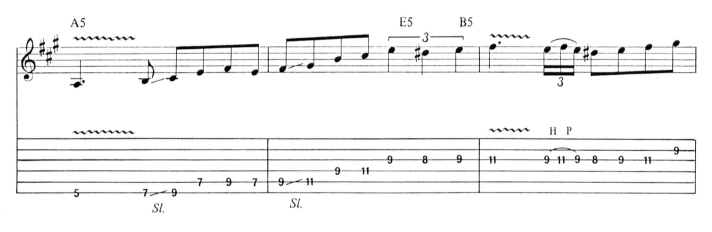

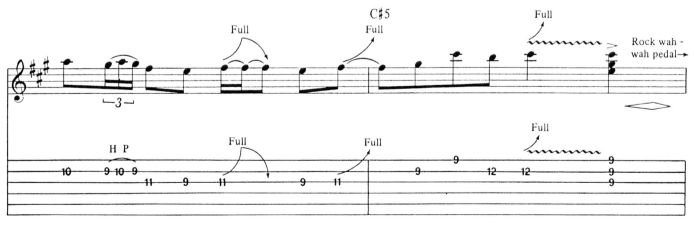

On and On

Words and Music by Michael Schenker and Gary Barden

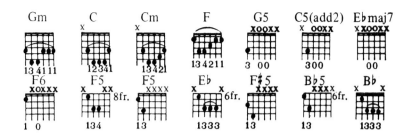

Poco rubato

Intro

(Polysynth. + string synth.)

Note: Guitar can simulate this line by
swelling each note with volume
control and vibrating each note ( )

(Lead guitar)

background

(Background guitar)
picking

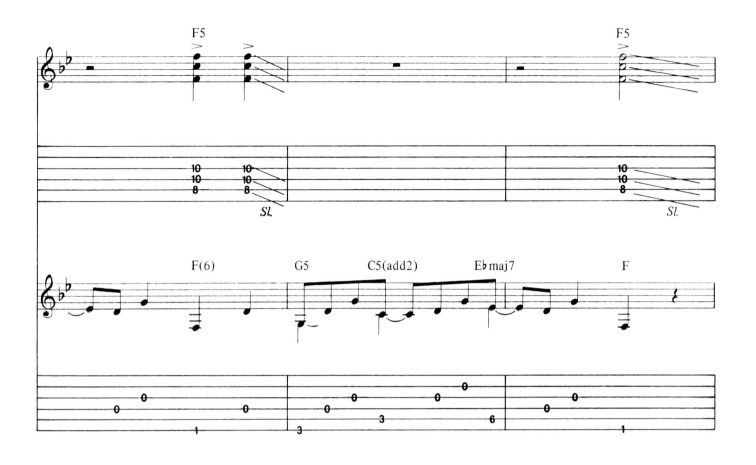

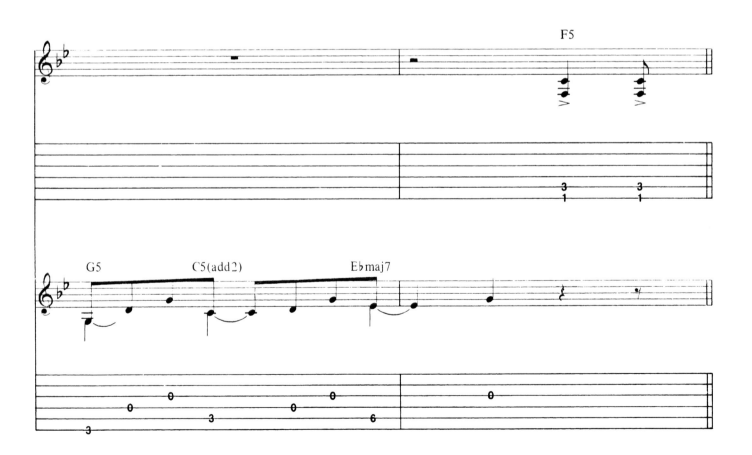

Verse

1.3. (A) kiss of the wind‿ when the spir - its let fly to the cold - ness of‿ the sun,‿
2. Blood on the streets,‿ when the black skies shout and then peo - ple cry‿ no more,‿

Fig. A

I got no place‿ to hide,‿‿ no - where to
dreams just fade‿ a - way,‿‿ re - al - i - ties

Fig. A

run. When the
soar. His

note: Long portamento bend
from C to F (P4)

Portamento bend

104

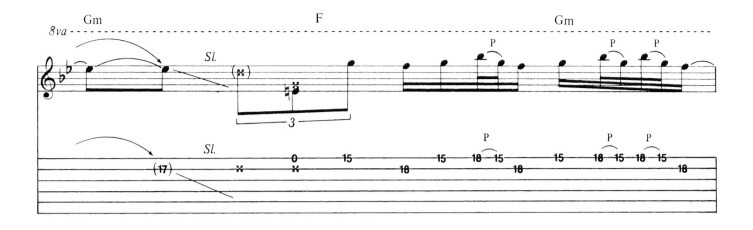

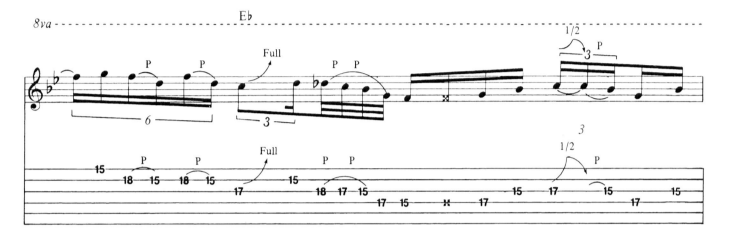

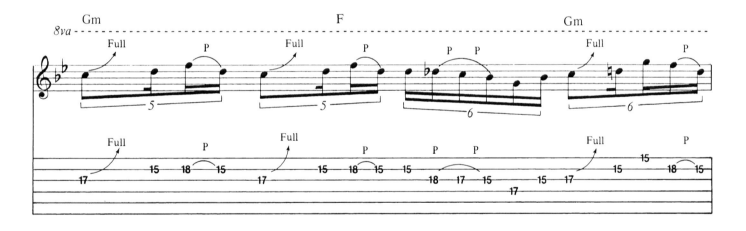

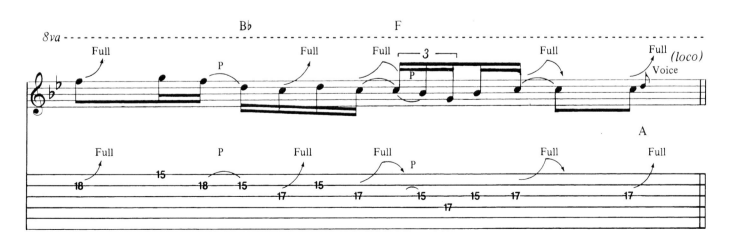

Guitar solo No. 2 (outro)

come. _____ On _ and on_ and on . . .

(Vocal vamp as background for solo)

Note: bend both strings . . . Finger ② string.
Do not pick ② string. Allow movement
of ① string to sound pitches of both strings.

Guitar solo No. 2 cont.

Rock Bottom

Words and Music by Phillip John Mogg and Michael Schenker

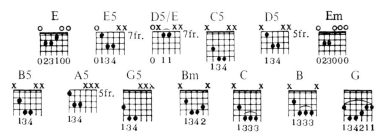

Medium Rock beat

Note: Mute all other strings: ④ thru ①

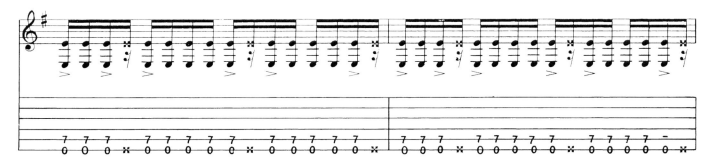

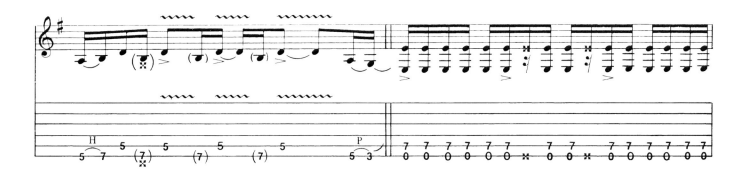

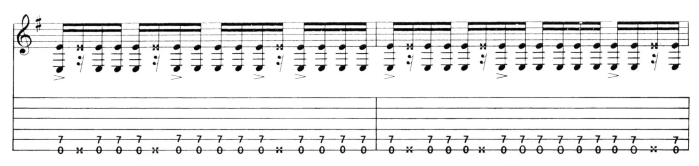

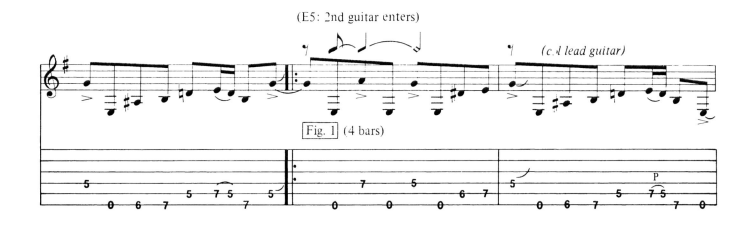

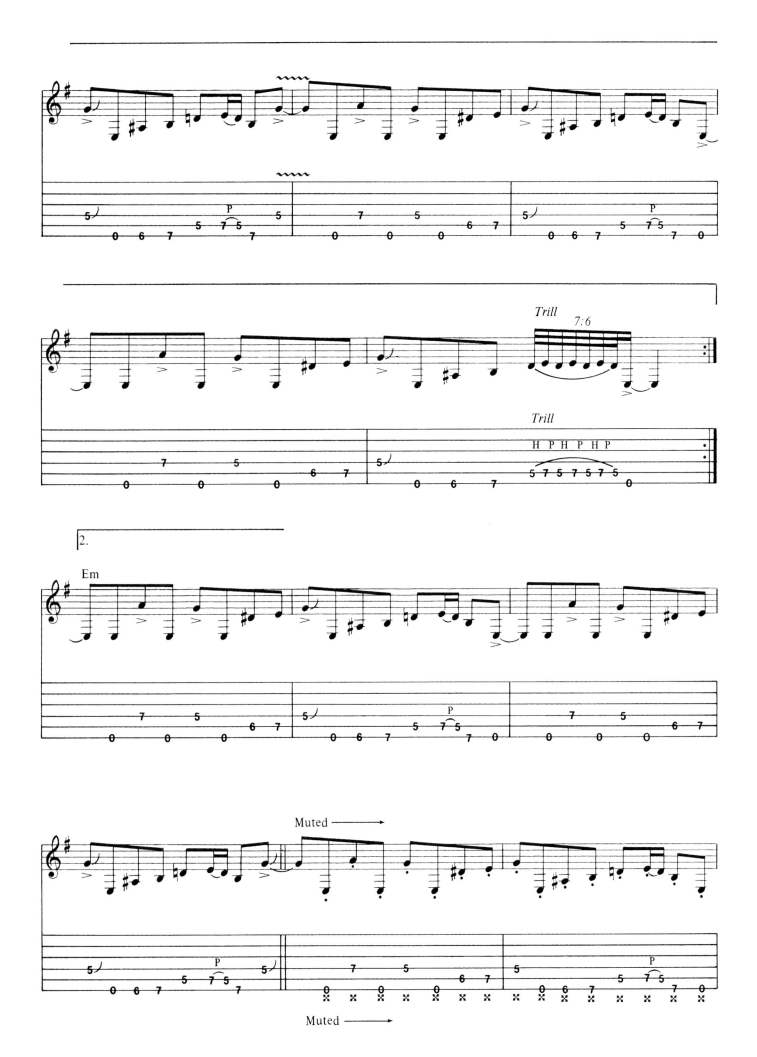

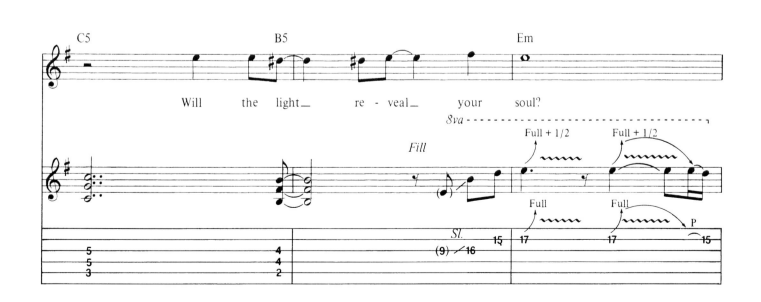

One— sweet kiss— on your

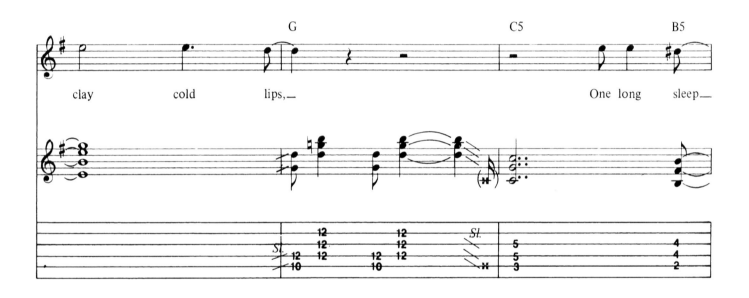

clay cold lips,— One long sleep—

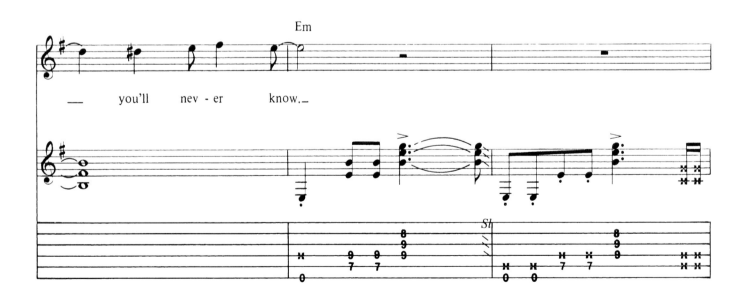

— you'll nev - er know.—

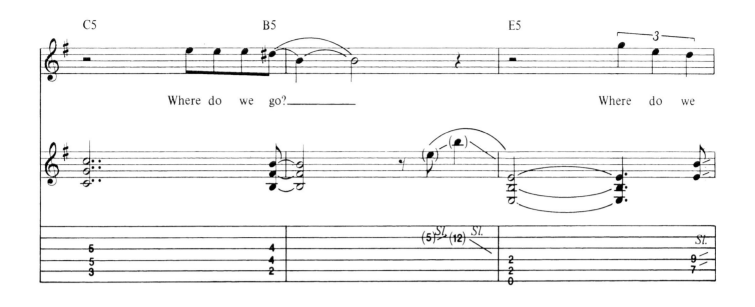

Where do we go?_____ Where do we

go? Where do we go_____ from

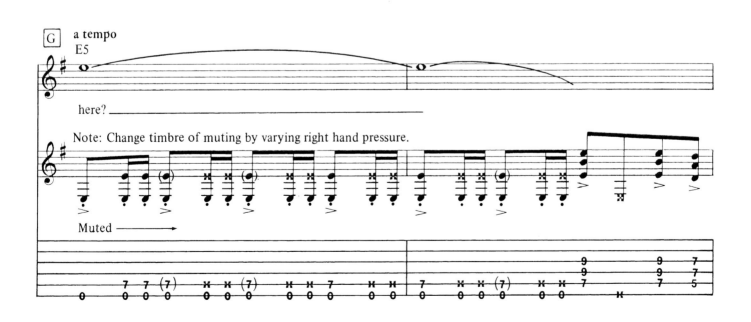

here?_____

Note: Change timbre of muting by varying right hand pressure.

Muted ⟶

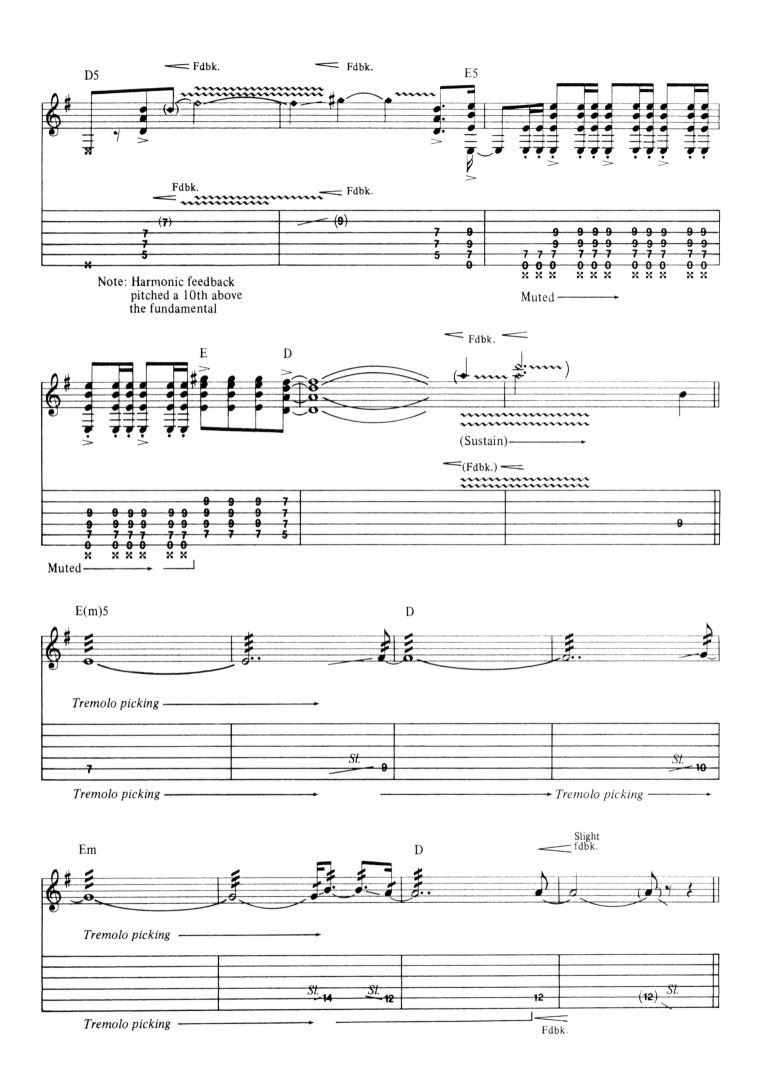

Guitar solo No. 1

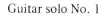

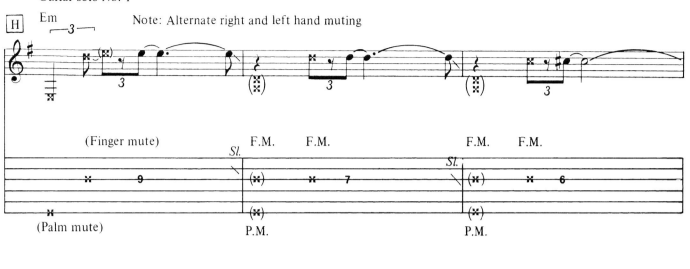

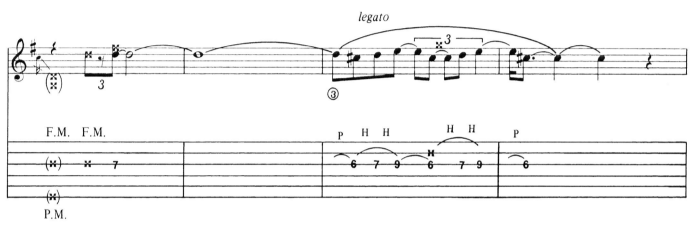

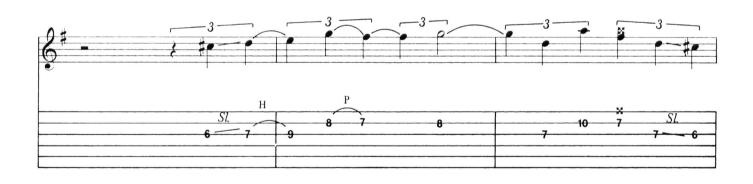

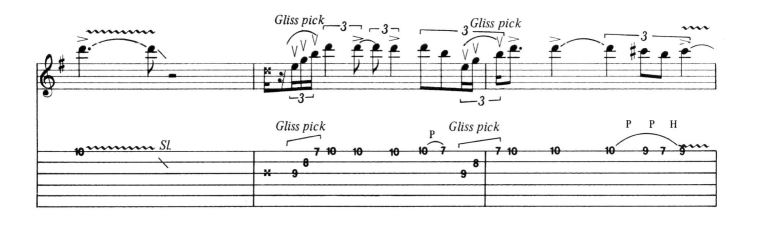

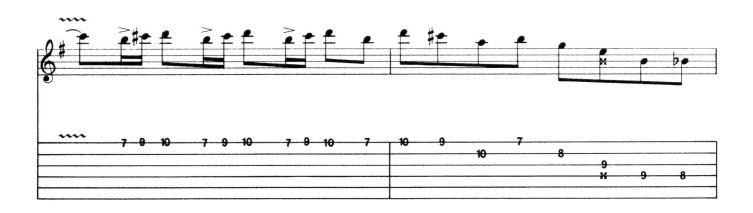

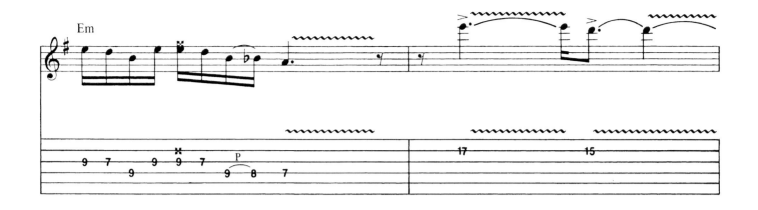

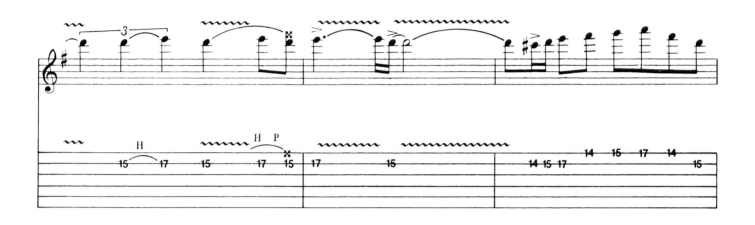

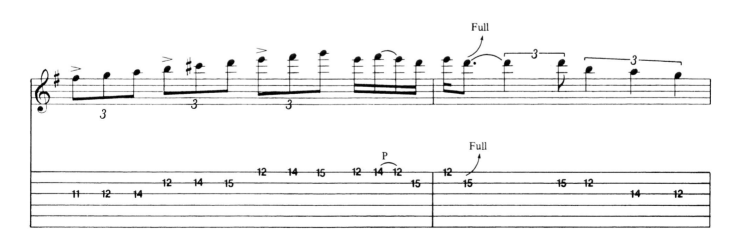

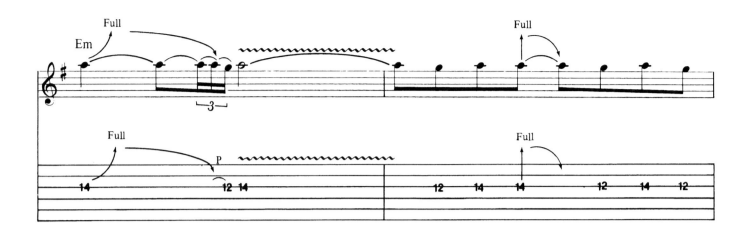

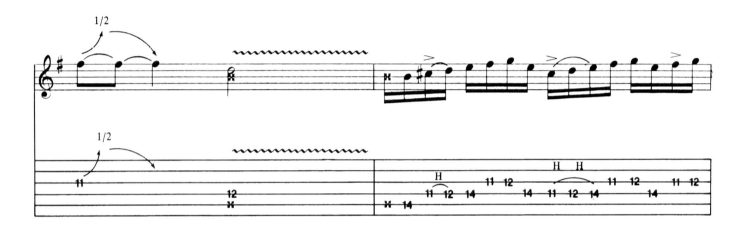

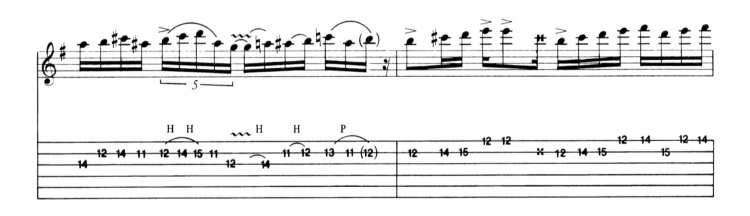

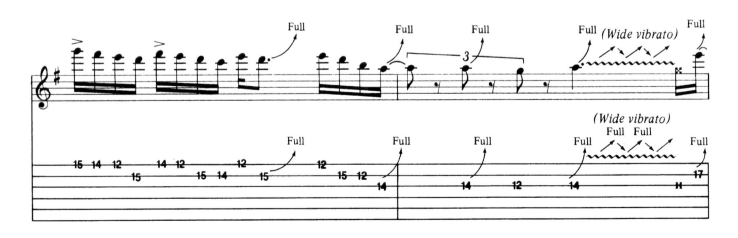

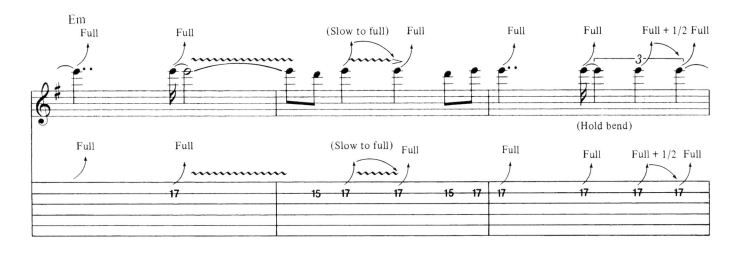

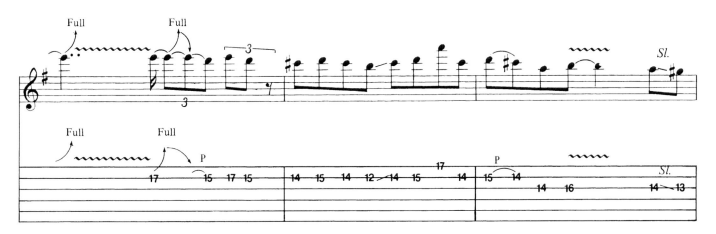

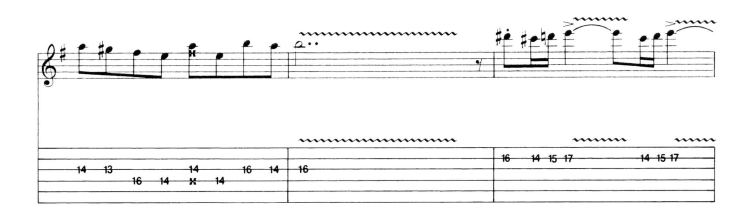

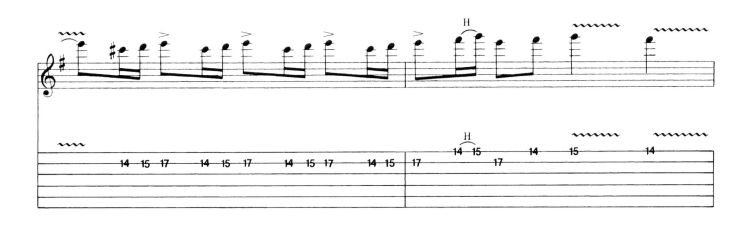

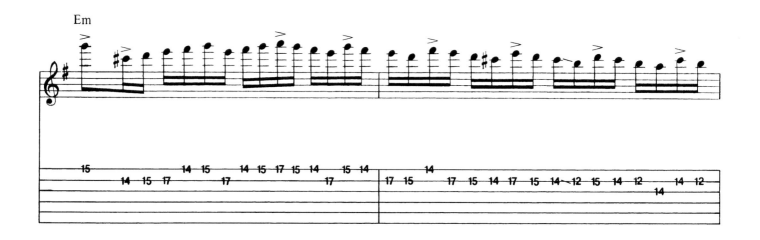

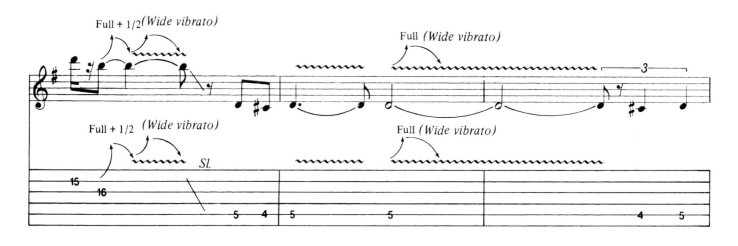

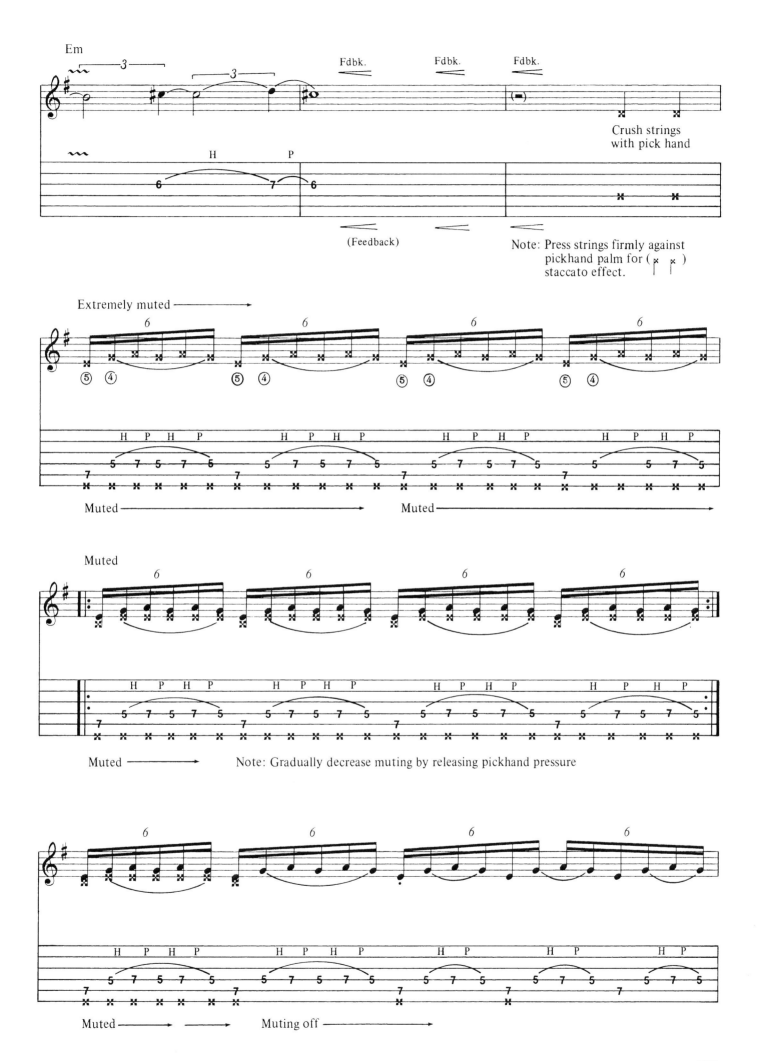

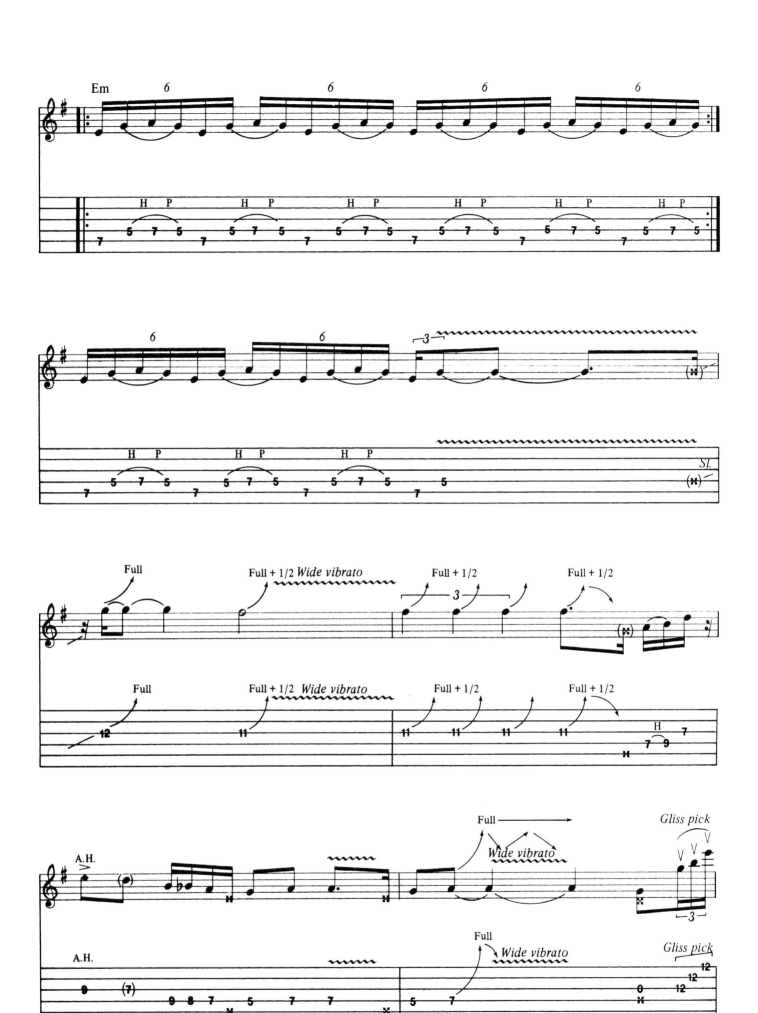

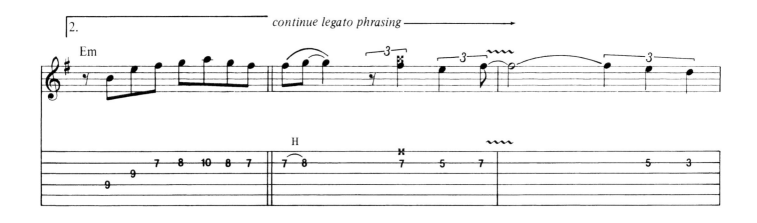

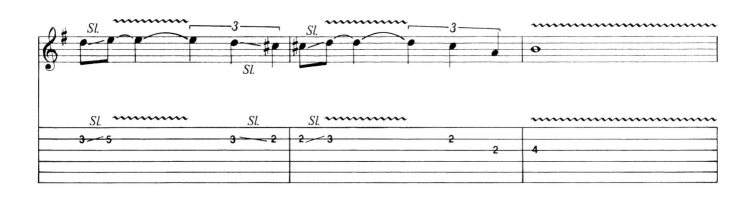

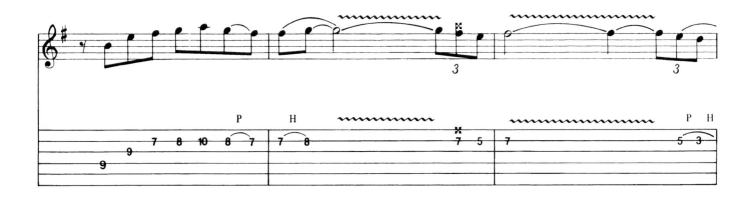

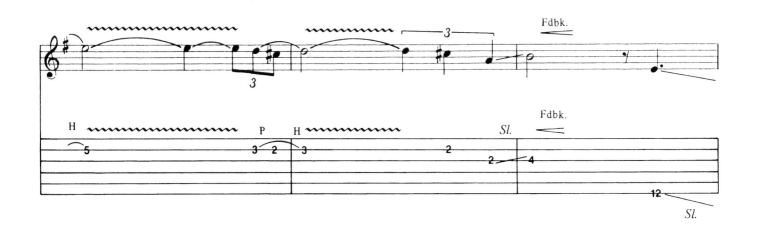

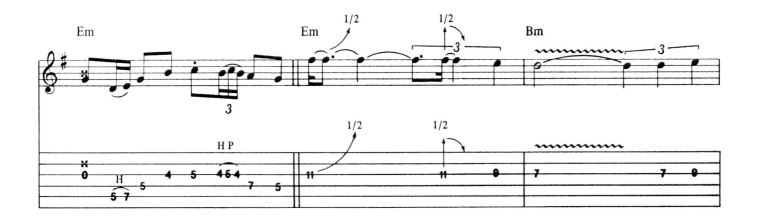

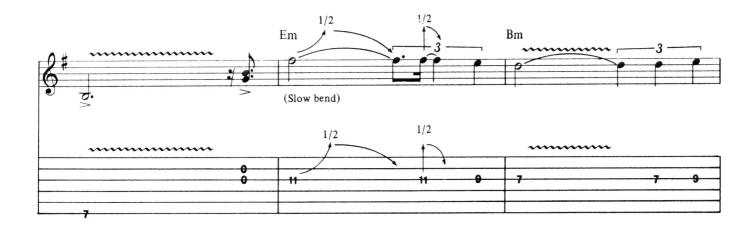

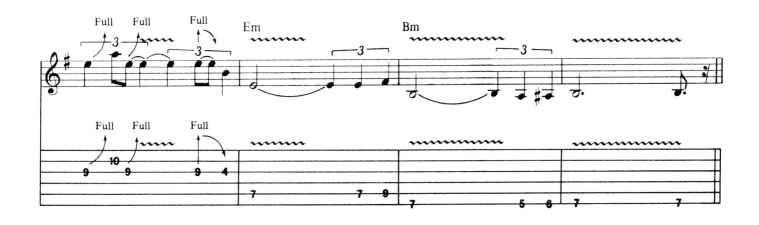

Guitar solo No. 2

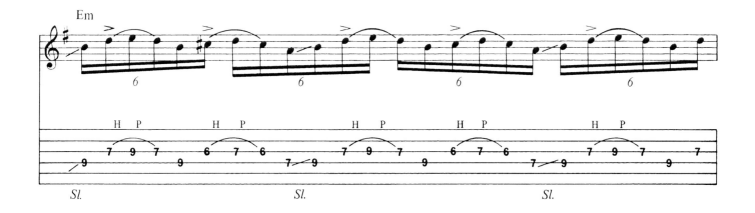

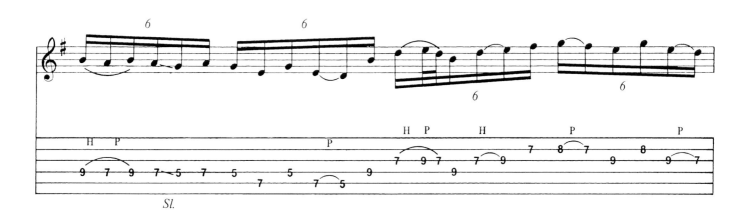

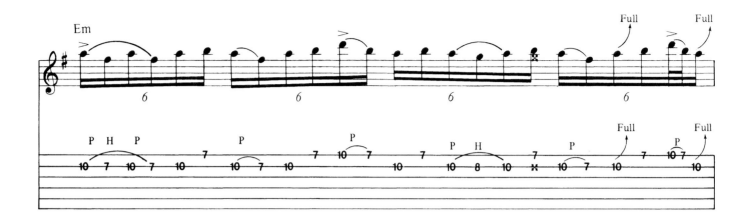

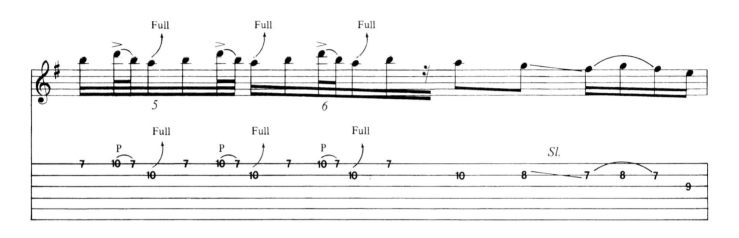

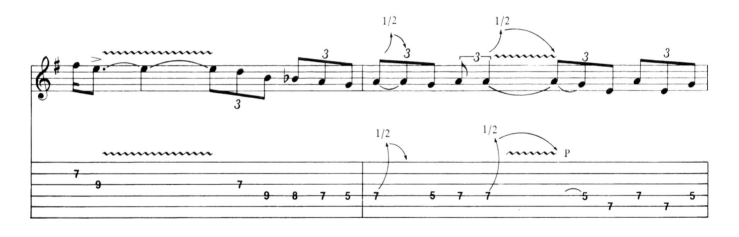

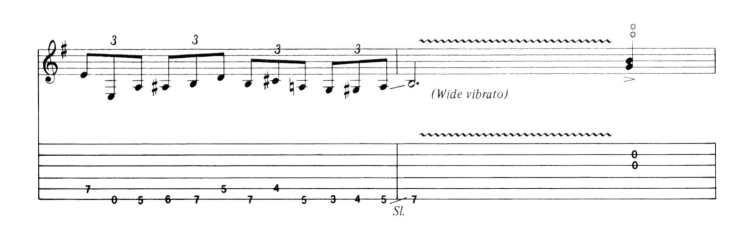

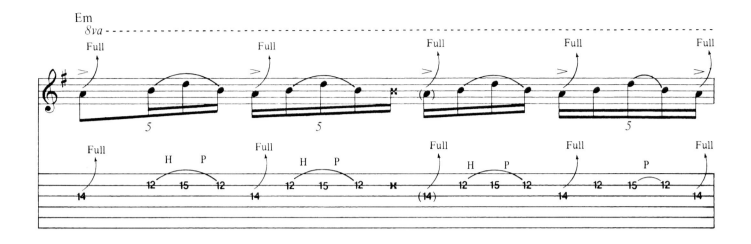

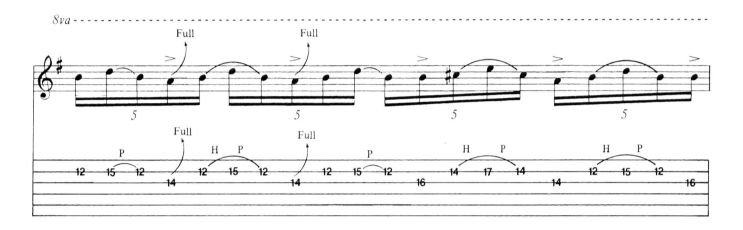

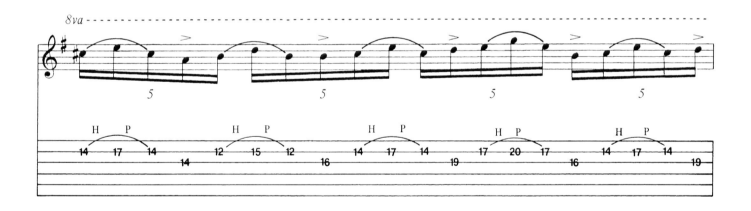

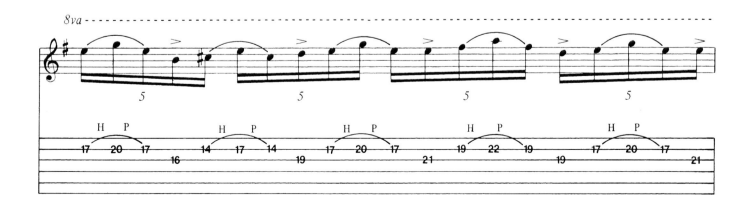

135

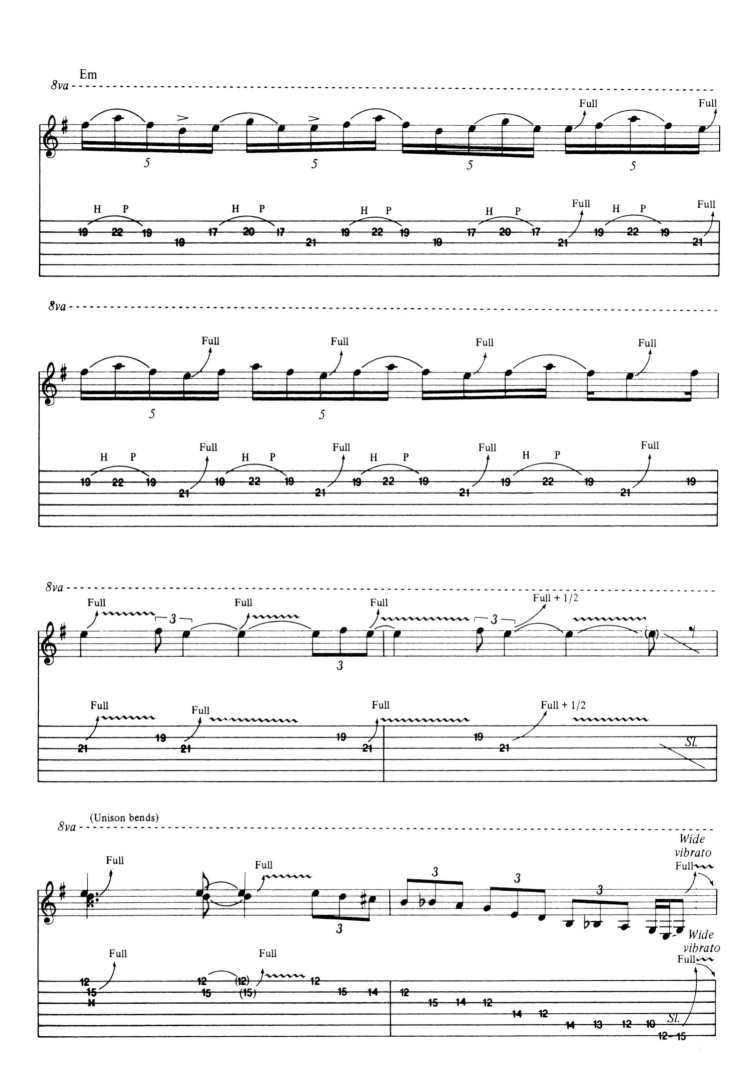

136

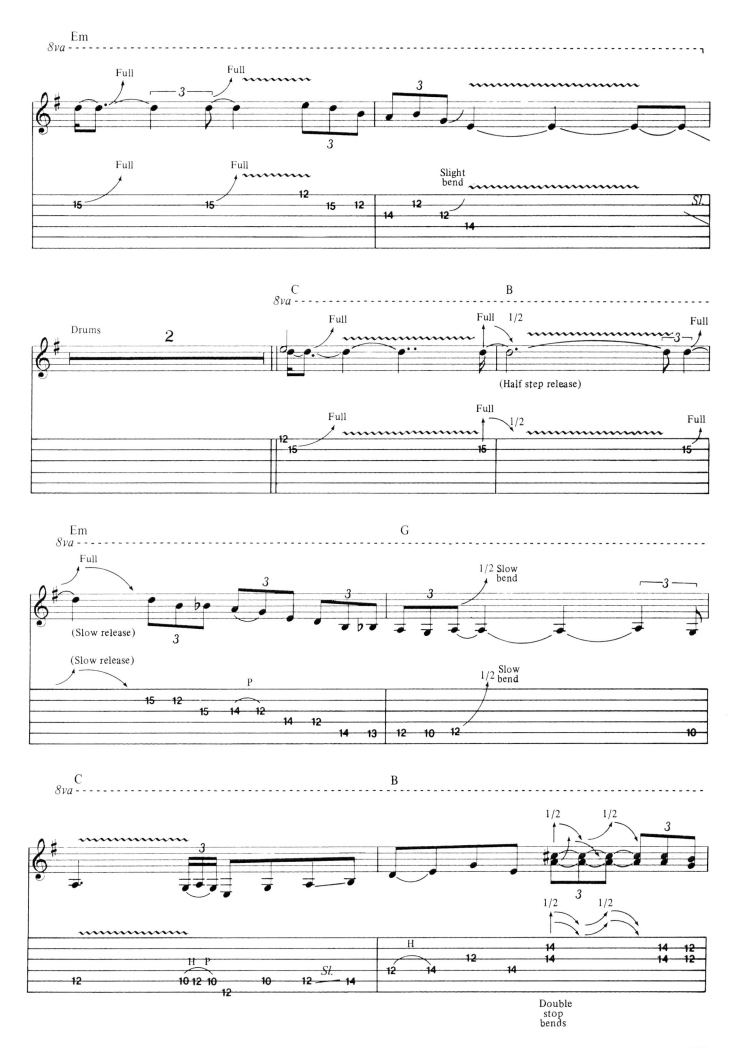

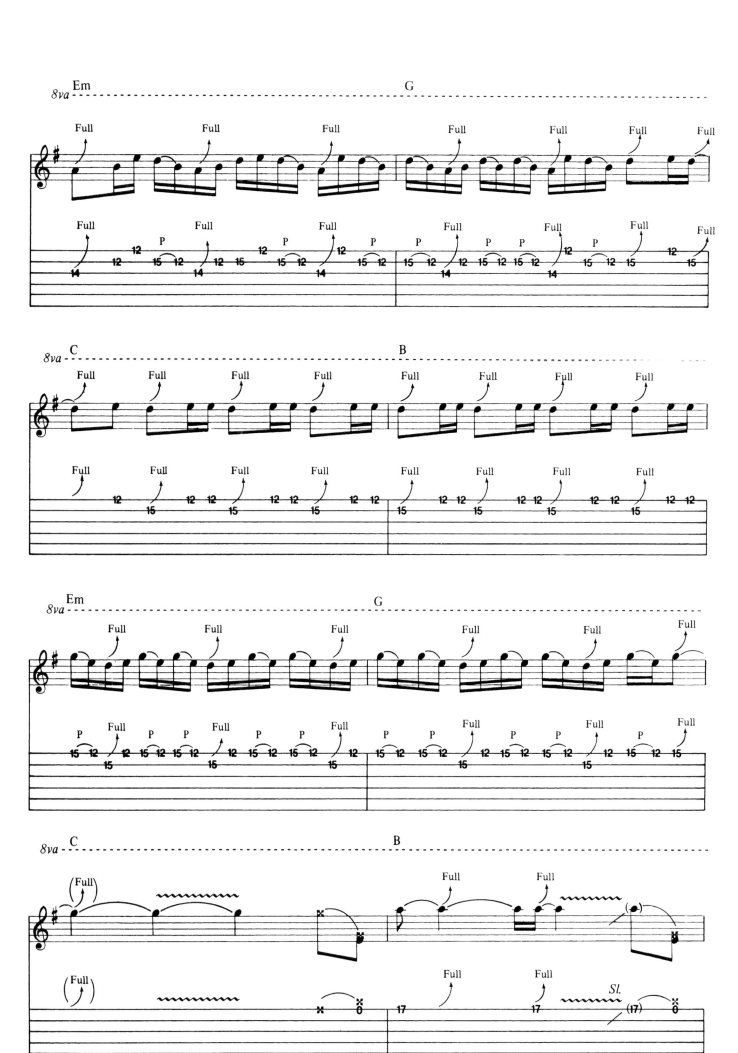

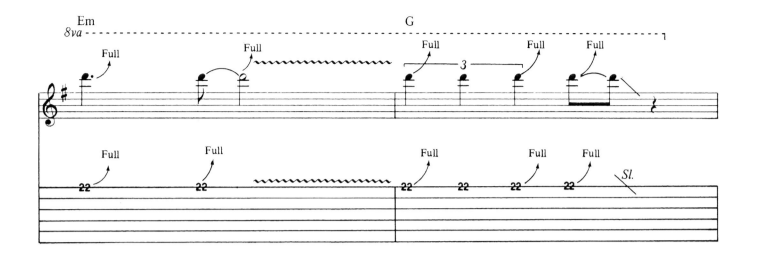

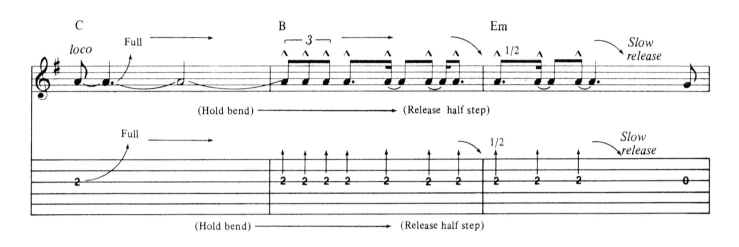

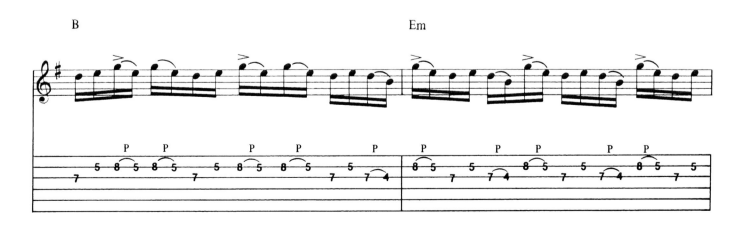

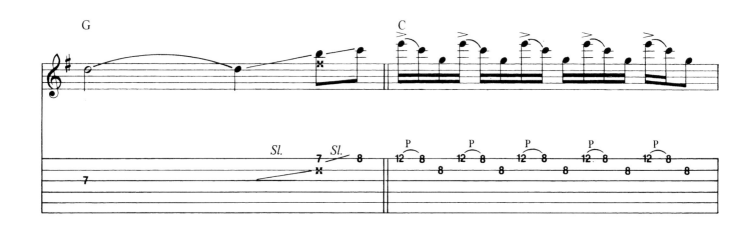

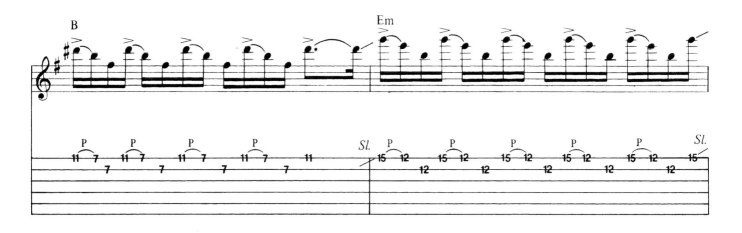

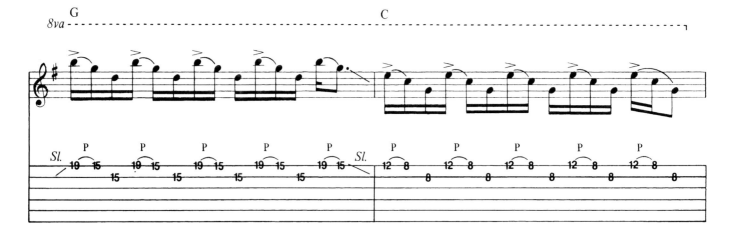

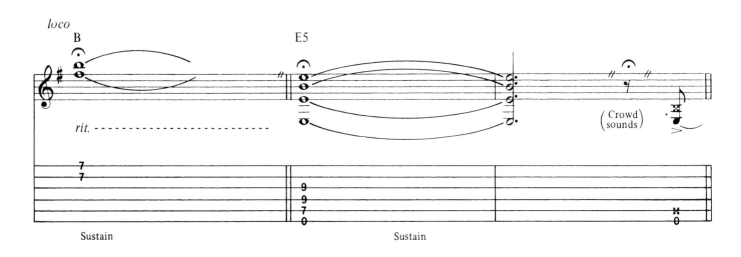

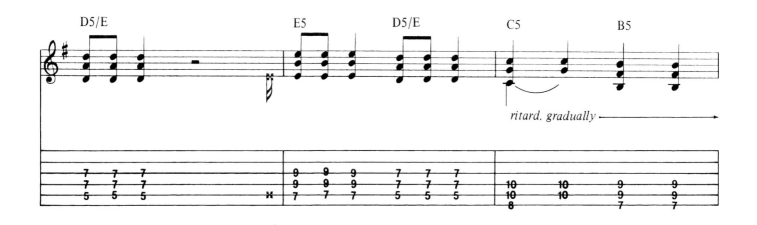

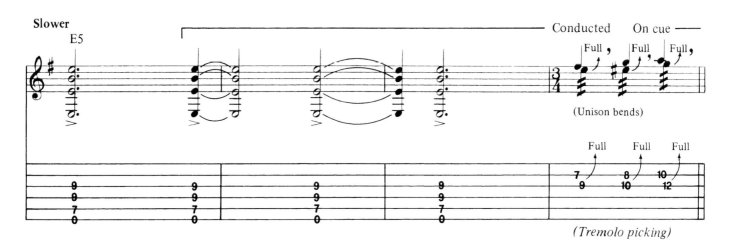

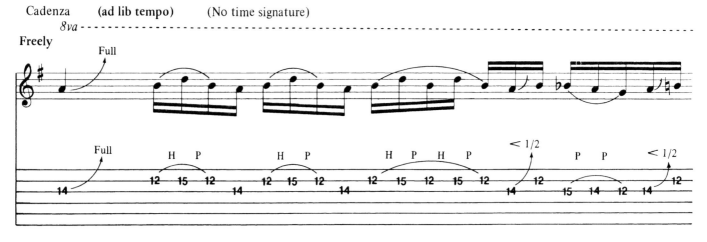

Note: Bends of less than a half step

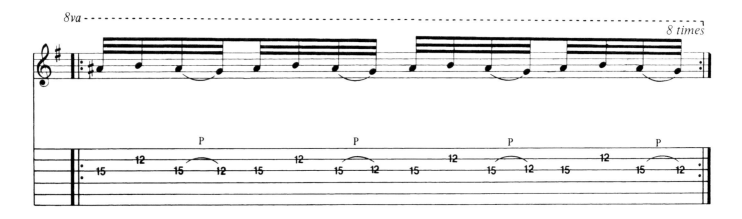

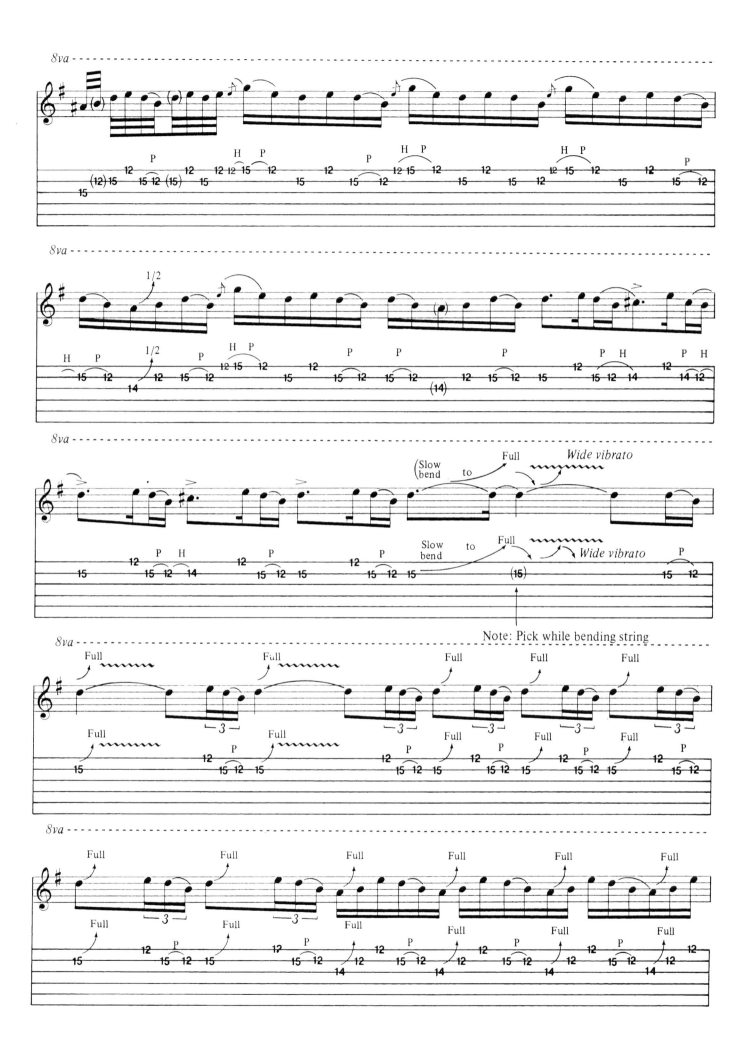

Rock My Nights Away

Words and Music by Andrew Nye and Gary Barden

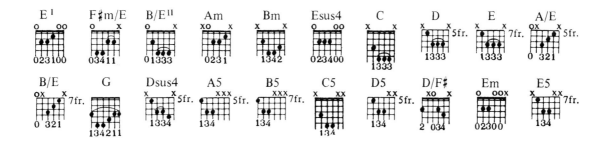

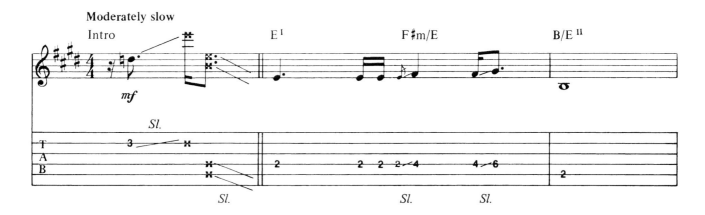

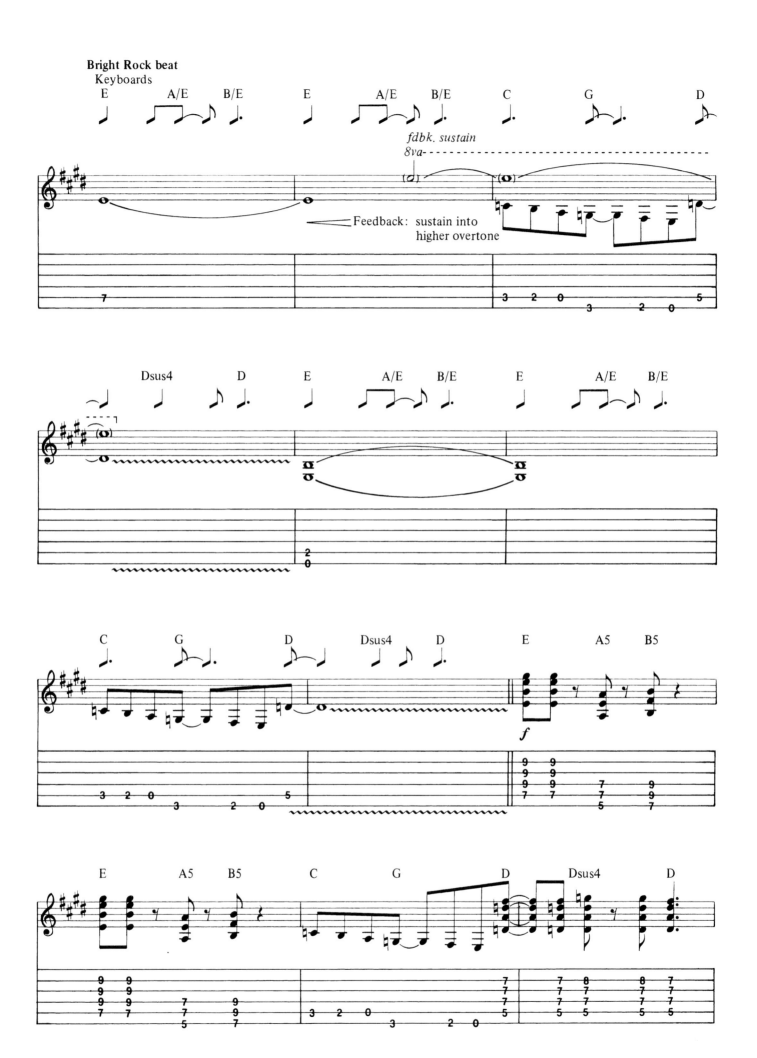

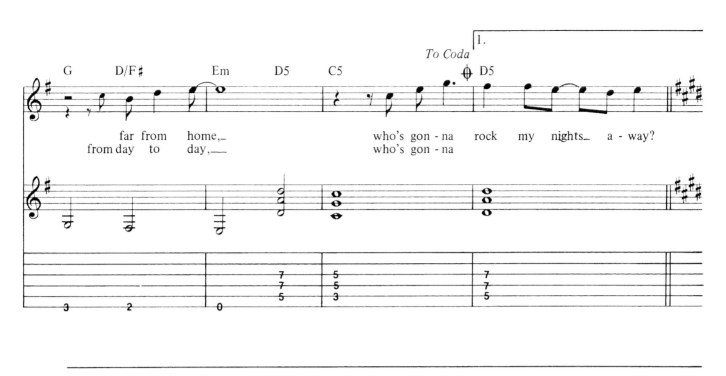

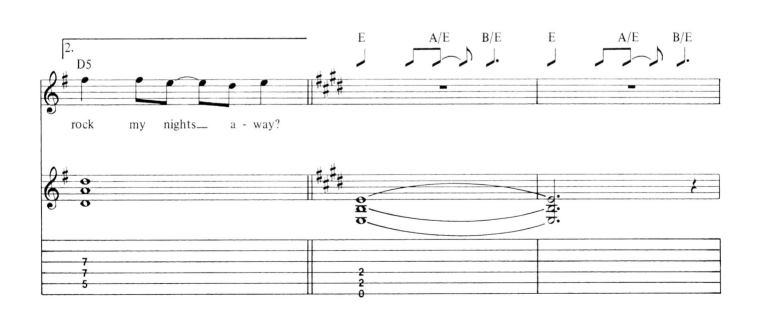

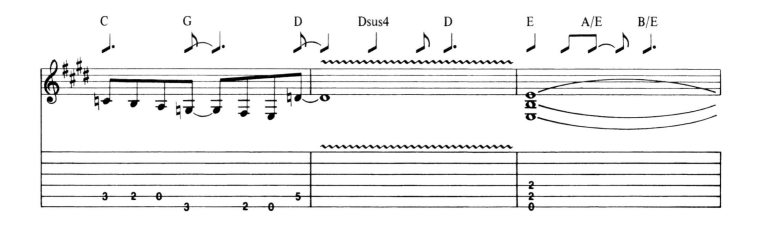

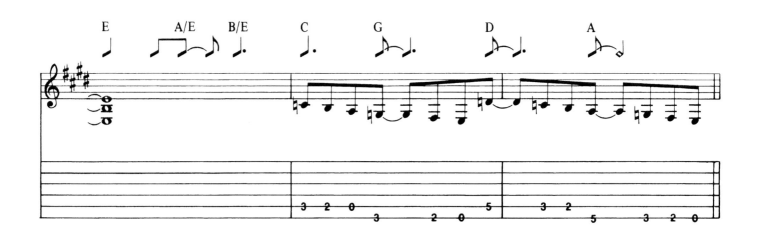

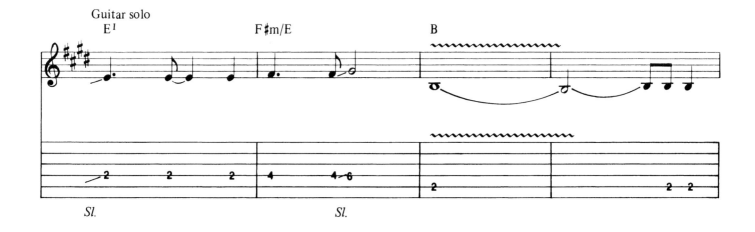

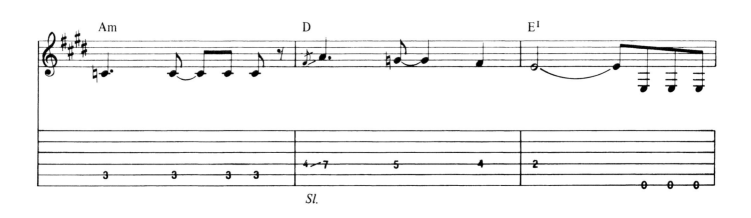

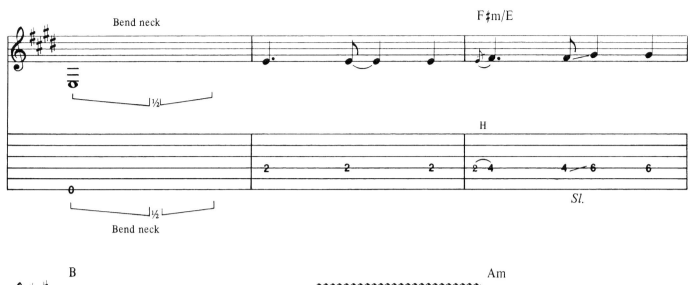

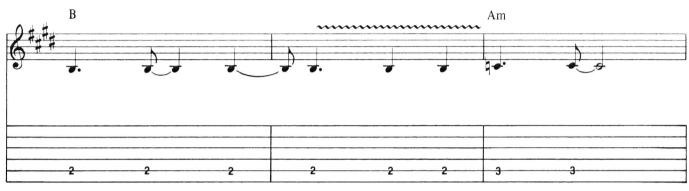

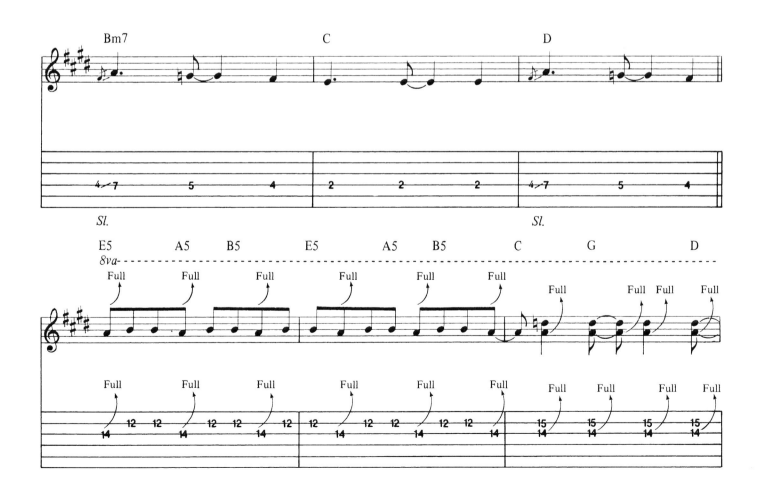

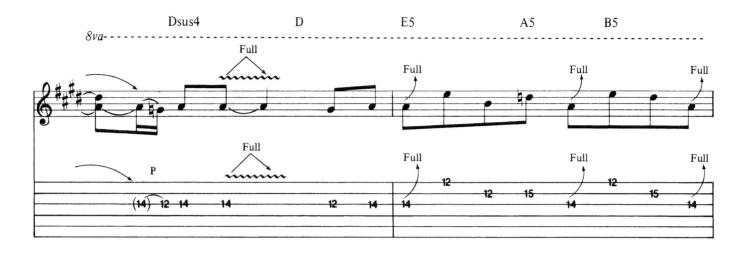

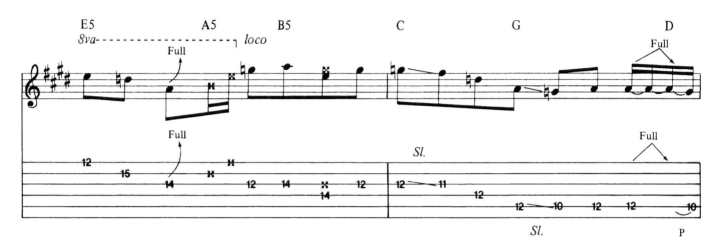

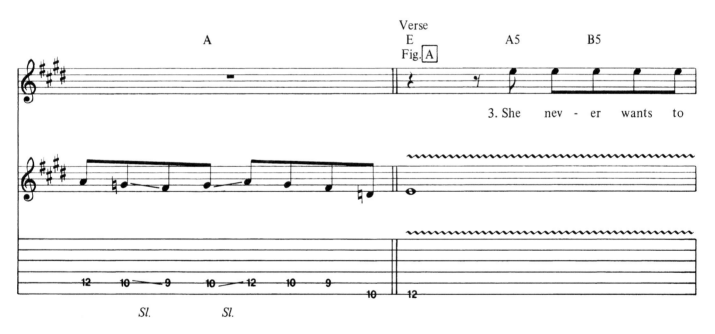

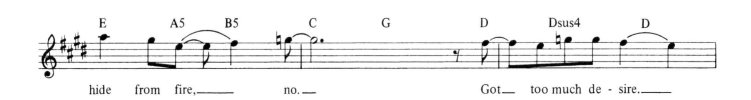

She's squeez - in' out the best in me,___ I know..

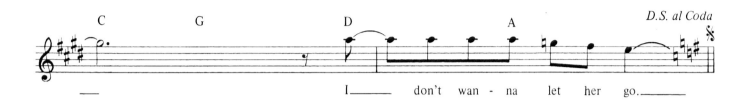

I___ don't wan - na let her go.___

D.S. al Coda

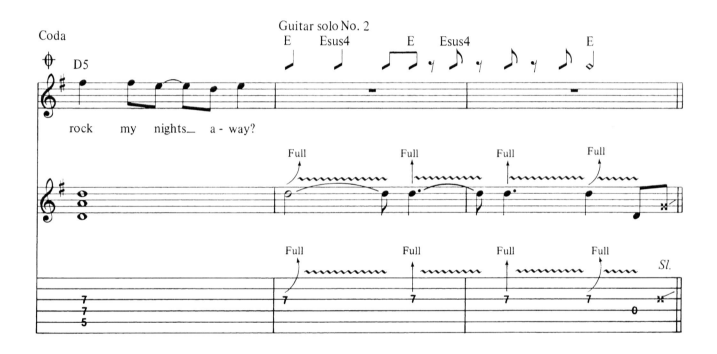

rock my nights___ a - way?

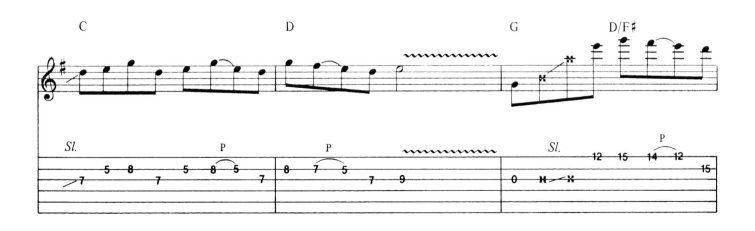

Save Yourself

Words and Music by Michael Schenker and Robin McAuley

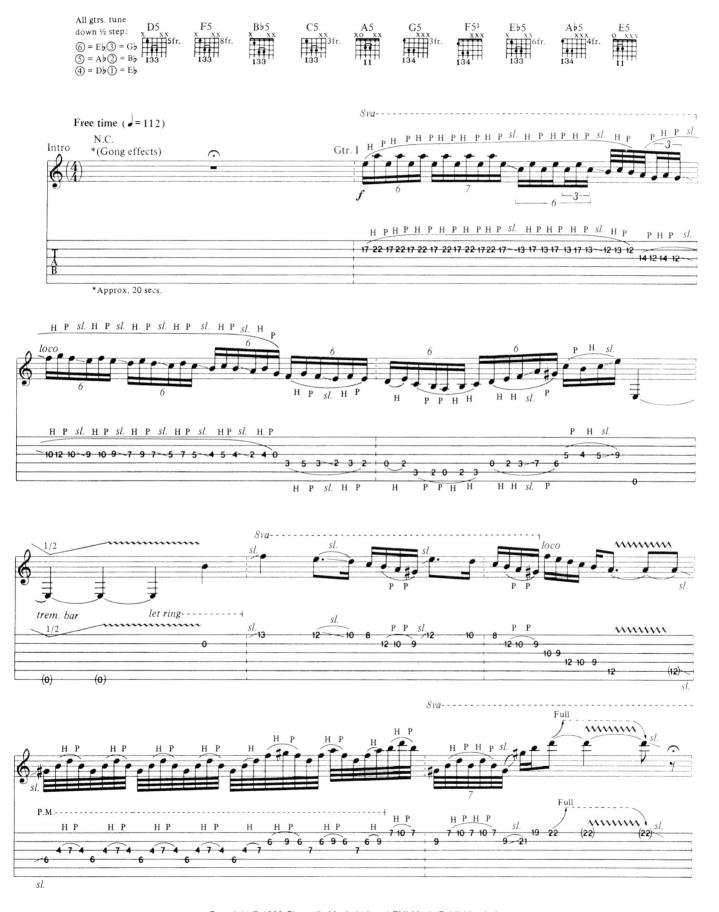

*Let open 5th stg. ring till next bar.

*pick slide

*Rapidly scrape pick back and forth
 while sliding.

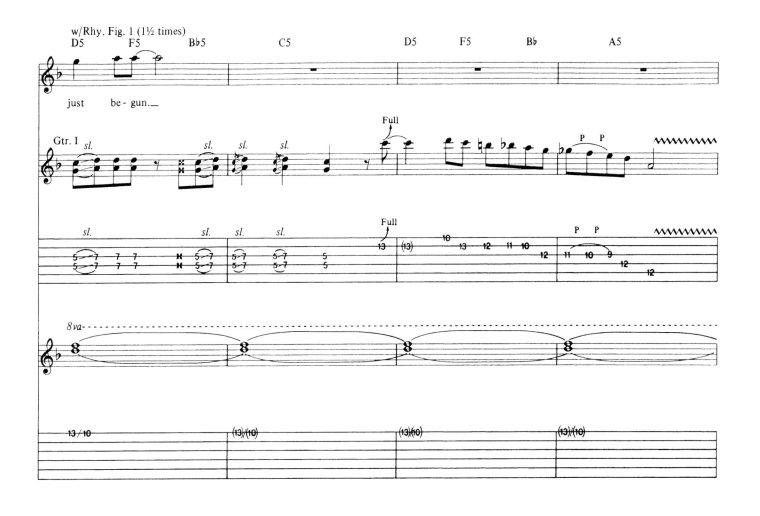

just be-gun.___

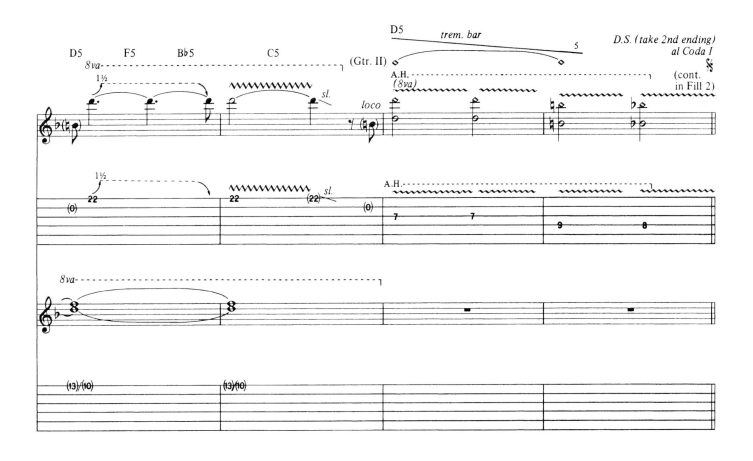

*Trills apply to both gtrs.*sl.*
**Gtr. V indicated to left of slashes in TAB.

*Vib. applies to both gtrs.
(next 10 bars).

*Hold last note of 5th bar for one bar (with vib.).

Additional Lyrics

2. Wind that beats across my face and rain that soaks my skin.
   Excitement that I feel down below and deep within.
   Each time I look at you, my little girl, I know it's true.
   I just can't help myself, can't stop myself all over you. *(To Pre-chorus)*

3. I've never known so much power since it all began.
   The Lord Himself must have touched me with His very hand.
   Such loveliness lyin' here before this troubled man.
   My little angel, spread your wings and fly me upside down. *(To Pre-chorus)*

4. *Sing 1st half of 1st Verse, then 2nd half of 2nd Verse. (To Chorus)*

TABLATURE EXPLANATION

TABLATURE: A six-line staff that graphically represents the guitar fingerboard, with the top line indicating the highest sounding string (high E). By placing a number on the appropriate line, the string and fret of any note can be indicated. The number 0 represents an open string.

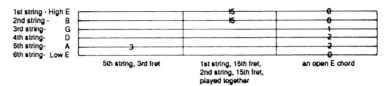

| 1st string - High E |
| 2nd string - B |
| 3rd string - G |
| 4th string - D |
| 5th string - A |
| 6th string - Low E |

5th string, 3rd fret   1st string, 15th fret, 2nd string, 15th fret, played together   an open E chord

Definitions for Special Guitar Notation

BEND: Strike the note and bend up ½ step (one fret).

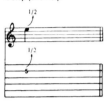

BEND: Strike the note and bend up a whole step (two frets).

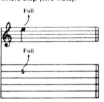

BEND AND RELEASE: Strike the note and bend up ½ (or whole) step, then release the bend back to the original note. All three notes are tied, only the first note is struck.

PRE-BEND: Bend the note up ½ (or whole) step, then strike it.

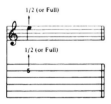

PRE-BEND AND RELEASE: Bend the note up ½ (or whole) step. Strike it and release the bend back to the original note.

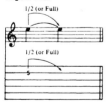

UNISON BEND: Strike the two notes simultaneously and bend the lower note up to the pitch of the higher.

VIBRATO: The string is vibrated by rapidly bending and releasing the note with the left hand or tremolo bar.

WIDE OR EXAGGERATED VIBRATO: The pitch is varied to a greater degree by vibrating with the left hand or tremolo bar.

SLIDE: Strike the first note and then slide the same left-hand finger up or down to the second note. The second note is not struck.

SLIDE: Same as above, except the second note is struck.

HAMMER-ON: Strike the first (lower) note, then sound the higher note with another finger by fretting it without picking.

PULL-OFF: Place both fingers on the notes to be sounded. Strike the first note and without picking, pull the finger off to sound the second (lower) note.

TRILL: Very rapidly alternate between the note indicated and the small note shown is parentheses by hammering on and pulling off.

TAPPING: Hammer ("tap") the fret indicated with the right-hand index or middle finger and pull off to the note fretted by the left hand.

PICK SLIDE: The edge of the pick is rubbed down the length of the string producing a scratchy sound.

pick slide

TREMOLO PICKING: The note is picked as rapidly and continuously as possible.

trem. pick

NATURAL HARMONIC: Strike the note while the left hand lightly touches the string over the fret indicated.

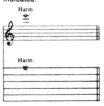

ARTIFICIAL HARMONIC: The note is fretted normally and a harmonic is produced by adding the edge of the thumb or the tip of the index finger of the right hand to the normal pick attack. High volume or distortion will allow for a greater variety of harmonics.

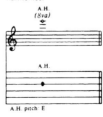

A.H. pitch: E

TREMOLO BAR: The pitch of the note or chord is dropped a specified number of steps then returned to the original pitch.

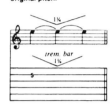

trem. bar

PALM MUTING: The note is partially muted by the right hand lightly touching the string(s) just before the bridge.

P.M.

MUFFLED STRINGS: A percussive sound is produced by laying the left hand across the strings without depressing them and striking them with the right hand.

RHYTHM SLASHES: Strum chords in rhythm indicated. Use chord voicings found in the fingering diagrams at the top of the first page of the transcription.

RHYTHM SLASHES (SINGLE NOTES): Single notes can be indicated in rhythm slashes. The circled number above the note name indicates which string to play. When successive notes are played on the same string, only the fret numbers are given.

Guitar Recorded Versions®

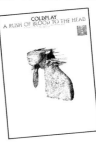

AUTHENTIC TRANSCRIPTIONS WITH NOTES AND TABLATURE

Guitar Recorded Versions® are note-for-note transcriptions of guitar music taken directly off recordings. This series, one of the most popular in print today, features some of the greatest guitar players and groups from blues and rock to country and jazz. Guitar Recorded Versions are transcribed by the best transcribers in the business. Every book contains notes and tablature.

AUTHENTIC TRANSCRIPTIONS WITH NOTES AND TABLATURE

FOR MORE INFORMATION, SEE YOUR LOCAL MUSIC DEALER,
OR WRITE TO:

HAL•LEONARD®
CORPORATION
7777 W. BLUEMOUND RD. P.O.BOX 13819 MILWAUKEE, WI 53213

Visit Hal Leonard online at www.halleonard.com
Prices, contents, and availability subject to change without notice.

0605

HAL•LEONARD® GUITAR PLAY·ALONG

This series will help you play your favorite songs quickly and easily. Just follow the tab and listen to the CD to hear how the guitar should sound, and then play along using the separate backing tracks. Mac or PC users can also slow down the tempo by using the CD in their computer. The melody and lyrics are included in the book so that you can sing or simply follow along.

INCLUDES TAB

Prices, contents, and availability subject to change without notice.

FOR MORE INFORMATION, SEE YOUR LOCAL MUSIC DEALER,
OR WRITE TO:

HAL•LEONARD® CORPORATION
7777 W. BLUEMOUND RD. P.O. BOX 13819 MILWAUKEE, WI 53213

Visit Hal Leonard online at www.halleonard.com

0305